A Leadership Strategy

"Dr. Downey's book is a must-read for any health care professional that is being on-boarded to a new organization. Her sequential leadership building blocks provide the reader with a step-by-step process for leadership development. I highly recommend it."

—Dr. Barry A. Doublestein, adjunct professor of healthcare leadership, Regent University, School of Business and Leadership

"The story told through Linda's experience is intentional and very effective at taking the reader through a journey of the highs and lows of leadership practices, leadership philosophies, and useful leadership lessons. I especially appreciated the sequential leadership building blocks to promote learning at the end of each chapter."

—Dr. Kathleen Cabler, ODCP, president and CEO, Cabler Consulting Group

A Leadership Strategy

Been There and Done That!

Dr. Sharon E. Downey, DSL

Copyright © 2020 Dr. Sharon E. Downey, DSL.

All rights reserved. No part of this book may be used or reproduced by any means, graphic, electronic, or mechanical, including photocopying, recording, taping or by any information storage retrieval system without the written permission of the author except in the case of brief quotations embodied in critical articles and reviews.

This book is a work of non-fiction. Unless otherwise noted, the author and the publisher make no explicit guarantees as to the accuracy of the information contained in this book and in some cases, names of people and places have been altered to protect their privacy.

Archway Publishing books may be ordered through booksellers or by contacting:

Archway Publishing
1663 Liberty Drive
Bloomington, IN 47403
www.archwaypublishing.com
1 (888) 242-5904

Because of the dynamic nature of the Internet, any web addresses or links contained in this book may have changed since publication and may no longer be valid. The views expressed in this work are solely those of the author and do not necessarily reflect the views of the publisher, and the publisher hereby disclaims any responsibility for them.

Any people depicted in stock imagery provided by Getty Images are models, and such images are being used for illustrative purposes only. Certain stock imagery © Getty Images.

Scripture quotations are from the ESV® Bible (The Holy Bible, English Standard Version®), copyright © 2001 by Crossway, a publishing ministry of Good News Publishers. Used by permission. All rights reserved.

ISBN: 978-1-4808-8592-9 (sc)
ISBN: 978-1-4808-8591-2 (hc)
ISBN: 978-1-4808-8593-6 (e)

Library of Congress Control Number: 2020901291

Print information available on the last page.

Archway Publishing rev. date: 1/31/2020

To my loving mother, Marian Riley, and to my family, Darrius Jenkins, Timmie Jenkins, Rodney Riley, Sheryl Lewis, John Riley, Theo Jenkins, Darrius Jenkins Jr., Ava Jenkins, Castiel Christoff Jenkins, Samantha Sturn, Khorey Stephen, Meghan Jenkins, Andrea Pearl Sison Jenkins, Trivon Lewis, Eddie Lewis, Shonda Lewis, Monica Riley, Nyisha Riley, John Riley Jr., Michael Lewis, Patrick Lewis, Louise Mills, Phillip Madison, Keith Madison, Keisha Madison, Loretta Bell, Valencia Oglesby, Bruce, and Kennedy Corbitt.

Preface

Leadership is not something new within society. It has been around from the beginning of time. This book came into existence as a result of my personal experience with unethical leadership. I had a difficult time with managers professing to do the right thing only to do the opposite when others were not watching them. I had experiences with managers who were position driven, with the intent of making things happened for themselves and not caring about their team. I also had experiences with organizations promoting core values while their managers did not adhere to them.

Why not? If managers are not doing the right thing, they cannot expect their teams to do the right thing. However, in healthcare (as well as other business sectors), integrity is necessary for leadership effectiveness. Having it can produce optimal outcomes for teams. After being in a leadership role for many years, I became convinced that ethical leadership is slowly slipping away—and that no one is noticing. In fact, it appears that managers who exhibit unethical behaviors are becoming tolerated and accepted. It is time to have a conversation about leadership.

Acknowledgments

Father God, thank you for all you have done in my life and through my life. I would like to thank everyone who played a role in my leadership growth and development. Without your love and support, it would have been impossible.

Dr. Floyd B. Willis, MD
Dr. Barry A. Doublestein, DSL
Ajani Dunn
Hannah White
Cynthia Bertagni
Betty J. Thomas
Mary Seabert
Anne Doyle
Carol Madison
Janine Samuel
Althea Gale
Doriel Gale-Corley
Jessica Bress
Raymond and Belinda Johnson-Cornett
Monte J. Reynolds
Mandy Lopez
Ruth Delgardo
Vernita Delgardo
Dennis and Gertha Deverteuil
Dr. Scott Arnold, DPT
Wanda Archer
Dr. Kathleen Cabler, ODCP
Lashanda Marshall
Linda Horne

Contents

Preface ix
Acknowledgments.. xi
Introduction xv

- Chapter 1   Leadership Position vs. Process: What Does It Mean? 1
- Chapter 2   Having a Leadership Mindset 10
- Chapter 3   Leadership Development: Mentoring, Coaching, and Consulting 24
- Chapter 4   Leadership Effectiveness 45
- Chapter 5   Measuring Leadership Effectiveness and Efficiency 63
- Chapter 6   Challenges in Leadership 81
- Chapter 7   Diversity in Leadership 101
- Chapter 8   Faith in Leadership 119
- Chapter 9   Pearls of Leadership 139

Bibliography 155
Appendix 169

Introduction

Everyone deserves a chance to be under the best leader in the world, or at least to have a chance to observe effective leaders in action. Somehow, leadership, even in some of the most successful organizations and societies, has lost its true meaning. Modern-day leaders are struggling with leadership identity (how they see themselves as leaders), which, in turn, prevents them from being effective and causes them to miss becoming a role model for their communities. Leadership as a whole has become a question: Do leaders really care about their leadership identity? Or are they just moving closer to the top of an organization, toward an invisible arriving point? Whatever the case, all leaders can make the best of their roles, pursuing moments and ways to make adjustments in their leadership style to achieve desirable outcomes.

As we look within organizations and society, there is a major necessity for ethical leadership. It is time to stop complaining about the lack of ethical leadership and to start doing something about it. This begins with the leader in the mirror. Do you agree with that statement? As individuals, do we know how to identify ethical leadership? Do we know how ethical leadership occurs? Who is ultimately responsible for ensuring ethical leadership? The answers to these questions—along with a creative strategy for leaders to become effective in their current roles—are emphasized in this manuscript. Additionally, individuals must realize that leadership is an ongoing journey. Proper leadership can change individuals' perceptions and behaviors along its pathway.

Throughout the manuscript, the author provides real

examples of her leadership journey, through a character named Linda. The stories are true, based on the author's experiences. The author changed names and some details in the stories to protect people's privacy.

On December 8, 2000, Linda—a supervisor in the field of healthcare—found herself in a difficult situation after supervising her team. She had made a decision to ensure patient safety, which meant her team had to respond to all emergencies promptly. Upon entering an emergency situation, Linda noticed that certain team members did not respond after getting a notification. She decided to call each team member about his or her absence from the emergency. Linda received resistance from a few team members after questioning their actions. The team members decided to report Linda's questioning to her boss, succumbing to "first person who tells the story wins the prize" syndrome. Linda was reprimanded by her direct boss after she questioned her team members, with the goal of ensuring patient safety. Linda was not given a chance to explain the incident even though she was ultimately responsible for the patients and staff. Her boss found her guilty, sending the message that the staff's opinion was more important than hers as a leader. Linda decided to write a note to her boss to explain her side, since he was not actively listening to her.

The author's note (reprinted with permission) read as follows:

> In response to the recent incident based on a decision that I made while being in a leadership role, I wanted to share my standpoint. I was performing this job to the best of my abilities and in accordance with the way I have been taught to do this job. The outcome of this incident has led to animosity between my team and myself, which then led them to approach management with this unfounded and ridiculous accusation.

I only approach them about problems which could impact the patients and them as well. I feel that I have received no support from you as a leader when it was appropriate. This lack of support has led me to conclude that there is no respect for the position in which you felt that I was qualified to obtain. This position carries an enormous amount of responsibilities that could result in the leader willingly accepting the blame for things that go wrong during their leadership role, and I accept that challenge.

Linda concluded the note, "Thank you for your consideration." As a leader, do you think individuals should be expected to supervise and be placed in a position with a lack of support from their direct leaders? Linda's experience was an eye-opener for her as an emerging leader. She began a quest to understand leadership, seeking leaders who were truly talking and walking in ethical leadership, keeping in mind that no individual is without his or her imperfections. However, all leaders have a moral compass; just using it can keep one off the path of self-destruction as well as prevent the destruction of others. The right leadership can bring out the best in people, and the wrong leadership can hinder their growth.

Chapter 1

Leadership Position vs. Process: What Does It Mean?

What Is Leadership?

People are obsessed with leadership, especially when established leaders fail to perform to an expected standard. *Leadership* takes on a different meaning for different individuals in society. It can be used to improve an individual's work and home lives, but there must be a basic foundation for its effectiveness in the long run. In fact, "leadership can be a personal journey and a process for change."[1] Northouse suggests that leadership can be complicated, and to understand it, one must approach it from different angles.[2] In fact, the closer individuals move toward leadership practice, the more clarity and understanding they will bring to their leadership identity.

Leadership is a process between individuals in authority,

---

[1] David A. Olson, "Are Great Leaders Born, or Are They Made?" *Frontiers of Health Services Management* (2009): 27.

[2] Peter G. Northouse, *Leadership: Theory and Pratice*, 6th ed. (New Delhi: Sage Publications Inc., 2013), 1.

people under those authorities, and the situation occurring among them. Northouse suggests that "leadership is present when a person(s) is persuaded by a certain individual in a group setting to reach defined objectives."[3] Leadership has many components, such as motivation, influence, loyalty, and trust of others, and an effective leader will eventually bring out the best in the team. John Lawn notes that "leadership is about inspiring others, and it is a crucial part that makes the difference between those organizations that have a competitive advantage and succeed and those organizations that are not growing or failing."[4] It does not matter which leadership role individuals occupy; there are areas of opportunity for everyone.

However, the leadership experience is ongoing. Leaders are faced with continuous learning and adaptation in their work and home lives. Their experiences can create future references for them to use in certain situations. Stephen Kempster says, "Leadership learning through experience draws on the complex milieu of events and influences that occur through daily interactions within particular contexts, and through these interactions, leadership meaning and purpose is developed."[5]

For instance, Linda's engagement with her direct leader and team provoked her to obtain a better understanding of leadership complexities. On a certain day, she reported to work only to find that she had been appointed several tasks by her peer—someone on the same level of leadership. She was informed by her direct reports that her peers had gone to lunch at a local restaurant and she had purposely not been invited. Other direct reports had overheard Linda's peers

---

[3] Ibid., 5.
[4] John Lawn, "What Is Leadership?" *Food Management* (2013): 6.
[5] Stephen Kempster, "Leadership Learning through Lived Experience: A Process of Apprenticeship?" *Journal of Management and Organization* (2006): 5.

discussing her. Yet Linda had to look at the bigger picture, ensuring that the flow of the shift was properly operating and the staff's needs were met.

Linda knew her team wanted a negative reaction, but she had learned that she was ultimately responsible for the office atmosphere. Linda decided to smile and say, "Please don't worry about it; we are going to have a good day!" She remained focused and positive, moving her team forward. Linda's reaction demonstrated an important leadership principle: regardless of the challenges, "leaders need to deliver results."[6] The following day, one of Linda's peers apologized to Linda for neglecting to inform her they were going to lunch. Understanding the qualities of leadership is the first step of a leadership strategy. It supports a leader's future growth and development. Linda had no prior education or understanding of leadership. However, she understood there was more to leadership than occupying a position.

Yet throughout the decades, leadership has changed its face and presented itself in different forms, requiring different attitudes from leaders. If organizations are to survive in turbulent times, there must be an observation of past, present, and future leadership needs within their culture and communities.

Leadership Faces: The Past, Present, and Future

Past   "The face of the past leadership was driven through imposing one's views on others for certain outcomes, leaders' traits behaviors were introduced, group approach was performed, and leadership was seen through relationships

---

[6] Emerald Group Publishing Limited, "Leadership Is about What We Deliver: Shaping Culture, Creating Patterns of Success," *Strategic Direction* (2014): 24.

Present "The face of the present leadership is adapting to change: Leaders need the ability to lead organizations change. It has been proven that more than 70 percent of the organizations have problems adhering to change."[8] "Leaders need to have the ability to support their employees by responding to stressful situations with openness, support, and compassion."[9]

Future "The face of leadership in the future starts with finding new ways of conceptualizing leadership and developing emerging leaders."[10] "Future trends will impact leadership through technology convergence, globalization, and scarcity of resources, etc."[11] "Leaders need to be flexible and adaptable with the ability to create and communicate a strategic plan to employees in a way that everyone is aware of the organization's priorities."[12] "Leaders must have the ability to inspire employees to perform at the highest level."[13]

creating the same interests among leaders and followers, leadership effectiveness was introduced."[7]

---

[7] Northhouse, 2.
[8] Joan Marques, "The Change Leadership Landscape: What Matters Today," *The Journal of Management Development* (2015): 1311.
[9] Ibid., 1312.
[10] Dimitra Iordanoglou, "Future Trends in Leadership Development Practices and the Crucial Leadership Skills," *Journal of Leadership, Accountability and Ethics* (2018): 118.
[11] Ibid, 119.
[12] Ibid.
[13] Ibid.

Leadership as a Position

Even with all the progress made in the study of leadership, there is still a common struggle with effectively leading others. Why? Tom Karp reminds readers that "whether leadership should be observed as a specialized role or as a shared social influence process is controversial in leadership theory."[14] However, some people confuse *having* a leadership role with leadership itself. In Linda's case, being in a leadership position a goal of hers from high school. She had participated in a health service aide (HSA) program during her junior year, and she discovered that she had some leadership qualities. Linda made a notation on her high school memory book page, entitled, "The Future," which read, "My future outlook is to attend a local community college for nursing. Then, to work on becoming a head nurse in a local hospital."

Thus, in Linda's early experience, after completing colleges courses in respiratory therapy instead of nursing, she found it simple to obtain a leadership position. She was offered such a position as she was mastering her current role as a respiratory therapist. She had become stagnant in that role, but she always carried out her responsibilities in an excellent manner. Linda made sure her patients' and their families' needs were met. For instance, she had a patient who was in the hospital on Valentine's Day, and she decided to purchase a card for him to give to his wife since he was unable to do it himself. The moment he gave his wife the card brought tears to everyone's eyes. Linda was excited about having a new position: it made her become more of a leader, or at least she thought it did. Linda had different responsibilities in the new role. Linda learned early in the transition that the new position did not define her; instead, she had to define the position.

---

[14] Tom Karp, "The Future of Leadership: The Art of Leading People in a 'Post-Managerial Environment," *Strategic Thinking and Policy* (2008): 31.

Despite her natural affinity for leadership, Linda met resistance when trying to lead others because she did not have the proper education and understanding when it came to leadership theory. One day, Linda's team did not have enough employees on staff for the amount of work ahead of them, and a team member told Linda abruptly, "You are a supervisor; get us some people." She remembered thinking, *But I also am a human being with feelings.* Linda realized then that she needed a strategy for leading others. "One goal of leadership practice is to create a way to make sense and direction of organization life,"[15] says Karp and Helgo—this means finding a way to work with differences of perspectives and to be effective in all interactions. "The dominant assumption among practitioners and leadership scholars seems to be that leadership is both desirable and necessary."[16] Most people consider the position to be beneficial: "leadership itself is a good thing and most employees benefit from and desire it."[17]

Linda decided to allow herself to drive the position and not let the position drive her or those under her authority. For instance, Linda stopped micromanaging others, and she allowed others to have input into decisions that affected them. Linda invested in herself through mentorship and leadership-development education. She had mentors in both her personal and professional life, understanding the need for mentors to become proficient in leadership. Linda was aware that leadership is not a position but a process, and this allowed her to lead others in the future. In fact, as Hooiiberg et al. note, "Effective leadership requires having a clear set of values for the position."[18]

---

[15] Karp and Helgo, 31.
[16] Mats Alvesson and Martin Blom, "Less Followership, Less Leadership? An Inquiry into the Basic but Seemingly Forgotten Downsides of Leadership," *M@n@gement* (2015): 266.
[17] Ibid.
[18] Robert Hooijberg, Nancy Lane, and Albert Diverse, "Leaders Effectiveness and Integrity: Wishful Thinking?" *International Journal of Organizational Analysis* (2010): 59.

Leadership as a Process

Melissa Horner reminds scholars that "the study of leadership over time has been performed in different contexts and theoretical grounds."[19] She continues: "Even though it has been observed as a process, most theories and research on leadership concentrates on an individual to gain understanding."[20] Maranthe et al. add that "leadership is the process of influencing others to understand and agree about what needs to be done and how to do it, and the process of orchestrating individual and group efforts to achieve common goals."[21] They envision leadership uniquely: "leadership can be compared to a triangle with its ongoing connective sides representing the leaders, followers and the shared vision."[22] Horne agrees with a connective vision of leadership:

The theory on leadership looks at leadership as a process in which leaders are not seen as individuals in charge of followers but as members of a community of practice, people united in a common initiative who share a history of core values, certain beliefs, ways of talking, and ways of doing things.[23]

Therefore, leadership is complex; it does not have a simple method that fits all situations in the same manner.[24] Silva reminds leaders that "leadership as a process occurs in a given context. If the context changes, the leadership process will also change."[25] However, "the concept gives the leaders, the

---

[19] Melissa Horner, "Leadership Theory: Past, Present, and Future," *Team Performance Management* (1997): 270.
[20] Ibid.
[21] Gaurav Marathe, Girish Balasubramaian, and Manish Singhal, "Demystifying The Leadership Kaleidoscope Into An Intergrated View," *The Journal of Management Development* (2017): 863.
[22] Ibid.
[23] Horne, 270.
[24] Alberto Silva, "What Is Leadership?" *Journal of Business Studies Quarterly* (2016): 1.
[25] Ibid, 3.

followers, and the context a very important role in the leadership process, all of them can impact each other."[26] The leadership process can be stressful if it is not properly managed by the leader. However, leaders must be patient and willing to trust the process.

For instance, On Easter night, Linda found herself in a difficult situation. She only for four employees to perform the same responsibilities of the usual eight employees. The issue was known by the leadership team as early as two days before. However, the team responded by saying, "Don't worry about it; Linda can deal with the problem." Linda had known that the task was a challenge, but she believed her team could perform at the highest level with only four employees. Linda decided to create a plan for the shift. She called a meeting with her team before starting. Linda told the team that she expected them to do an excellent job even though they were missing a few people and to perform each task in the spirit of excellence. The team appreciated Linda's communication before starting their shift.

Linda decided to reach out to other departments to help support their team. As a result, her team received a lot of support from their colleagues. Her team also had a positive attitude about working together. Linda made sure she was leading by example, taking an equal amount of the tasks along with her administrative work. The team appreciated her assistance. Linda had to foster a positive environment in a negative situation, and she went above and beyond to do so, ensuring each team member had a lunch break and even performing their tasks while they ate lunch.

As the night moved forward, Linda's team enjoyed their time together. They realized it was much easier working with four employees as opposed to the typical eight employees. Why? Linda had learned it was about balancing, setting the

---

[26] Ibid.,4.

tone, and the attitude of the employees in the triangle (or leadership process). Leadership as a process is similar to a triangle, with three connecting points: in this case, the points were Linda, the team, and the situation they faced together.

Summary: Building Block One

Being an effective leader requires a strategy. However, the foundation for the leadership strategy must start with having a clear understanding of leadership. That is the beginning of one's leadership effectiveness: knowing leadership with clarity. Leadership can mean different things to different people. In fact, leadership can be realized in a place where an individual can use one's own abilities to drive the position, or it can involve the engagement of the leader, followers, and their interaction, utilizing a triangle effect through connection. Leadership has changed its face over the years, and knowing how it changed is beneficial. In fact, to be competitive in their industries, organizations must understand the culture and community leadership needs in both the current and future state. They must be prepared by having the correct leaders, aligned with their needs, ensuring growth and success in others.

Chapter 2

Having a Leadership Mindset

Whether an individual considers leadership itself as a position or process, having a leadership mindset can influence their perspective. In fact, a leadership mindset produces the best outcome when it is needed during chaotic and situational events. Leadership allows leaders to choose their pathway, and they can change if it is not moving on a desirable route. The next step of the leadership strategy is to adopt a *leadership mindset.*

What Is a Leadership Mindset?

The ability to lead an organization affected by both internal and external factors requires a strategy. Being able to lead others through inspiration, coaching, mentoring, and developing them to their fullest potential requires a plan. Polboon et al. advise, "Strategic thinking can be viewed as a process of thinking about an organization and how to go about developing a strategy which includes vision, creativity, flexibility, and entrepreneurship."[27] Popular thought agrees that "it is a mindset and beliefs, as much as skills which separate the great leaders from the average leaders."[28] In fact, French argues it is the "understanding of a mindset that can improve an individual's capabilities to function in their leadership role, causing them to achieve goals, accessing their abilities and skills, strengthening an individual's attitude, and improving relationships within organizations."[29]

However, there are certain positive and negative categories in which an individual mindset (such as a leadership mindset) can be established. These include (but are not limited to) sociopath, egoist, chameleon, dynamo, builder, and transcender.[30]

Sociopath Mindsets

Cangemi and Pfohl note that

> The state of an individual not having a conscience is considered as sociopathy, and when the behaviors are demonstrated, such individuals are labeled sociopaths. Sociopathic thinkers act like chameleons in the beginning, deceiving most people, regardless of their experience or education level. Sociopathic thinkers are usually identified only after their damage and hurt

---

[27] Nuntamanop Polboon, Ilkka Kauranen, and Barbara Igel, "A New Model of Strategic Thinking Competency," *Journal of Strategy and Management* (2013): 245.

[28] Weblog post, Coaching Tips: The Leadership Blog: Leadership Mindset, (*Newstex*, Global Business Blogs, 2014).

[29] Robert French, "The Fuzziness of Mindsets," *International of Journal Organizational Analysis* (2016): 685.

[30] Modesto A. Maidique and Nathan J. Hiller, *The Mindsets of a Leader* (2018), 80.

have been done and they move on to another destructive path.[31]

Leaders with a sociopath mindset are seen as not having a desire or motive to serve anyone, which is a dangerous way of thinking.[32]

In addition, say Maidique and Hiller, "they are self-serving individuals, they lack empathy towards others' emotional and physical condition; they perceive self as superior."[33] Also, "they are usually charming and highly effective at manipulating others and the organization's system until they are exposed; they can exist at any level in an organization."[34] Leaders with a sociopath mindset will eventually destroy their character and an organization's credibility within its community.[35]

However, state Holt and Marques, "some of the areas of employment [where sociopaths are generally seen] are medicine, law enforcement, stock exchange, schools, universities, sales, advertising, and construction."[36] They go on to say that "employees under sociopath thinkers often feel less involved, appreciated, or rewarded. Sociopath thinkers do not like criticism and will maneuver business ventures into high-risk situations."[37] Sociopath thinkers also "perform unchallenged in their workplace, while they can cause devastation to their team, bringing the entire organization in which they work down."[38]

---

[31] Joesph P. Cangemi and William Pfohl, "Sociopaths in High Places," *Organizational Development Journal* (2009): 85.
[32] Maidique and Hiller, 76.
[33] Ibid.
[34] Ibid.,77.
[35] Ibid.
[36] Svetlana Holt and Joan Marques, "Empathy in Leadership: Appropriate or Misplaced? An Empirical Study on a Topic That Is Asking for Attention," *Journal of Business Ethics* (2012): 101.
[37] Ibid, 102.
[38] Ibid.,101.

For instance, Linda was scheduled to have a meeting with a certain leader and her colleagues. The leader had years of experience in a leadership role. The leader was known for his intellect and charming personality, always making those around him laugh and sharing the latest trends in technology. The leader had very little tolerance for others' personal problems, and he voiced his thoughts about others' issues openly to his peers or others in his space. Linda and her peers were scheduled to meet with the leader for a routine briefing. At that time, Linda decided to present a concern about one of her team members, who needed a schedule change because he had unexpectedly become a single parent. The team member was having a difficult time balancing work and home life and needed to transport his child to and from school since he did not have the support of his family.

Linda waited for the appropriate moment to bring up the topic, and she was stunned at the response. The leader yelled, " You can do whatever you want to do, Linda! I don't care." The leader's demeanor caught Linda off guard. She was not expecting him to react in such a manner. Linda was embarrassed by the reaction, which took place in front of her peers, but she had to remain focused and overcome that moment while ensuring the employee's need would be met. The leader never apologized for his behavior, but he continued sharing his plans.

In another incident, Linda recalled the same leader's behavior as abnormal. The leader decided to oversee a change initiative for the entire organization. The leader was boasting about how the change initiative would save money for the organization in the long run; he was excited and believable. However, when it was time to launch the change initiative, the leader went on a lengthy vacation, leaving the organization at risk to external vendors and failure. The leader purposely withheld information concerning the project. Linda found herself overseeing a project with little information. The leader returned from vacation only to find the project moving along successfully, and he became angry after hearing about Linda's progress.

Egoist Mindsets

Leaders with an egoist mindset are usually self-centered individuals, provoked by selfish ambitions. Debeljak and Kristijan state, "The word egoism can be viewed as an individual getting their own way, imposing their way of thinking, satisfying their own desires."[39] In addition, "they are stimulated by their own status of the position, wealth, social groups and power."[40] Leaders with an egoist mindset usually perform tasks with the intent of self-gain: *How can I profit from being part of the conversation or project?*[41] "Having an egoist mindset in a senior leadership role," Maidique and Hiller note, "can be detrimental to an organization's culture."[42] Egoistic conduct can hinder teamwork, preventing a team from moving forward in a successful manner.[43] Also, if an organization allows egoism to become a leading characteristic among its leaders, an atmosphere of unethical leadership may develop.[44]

Linda found herself surrounded by egoists in a leadership course at university. Most of the students were leaders within their organizations and communities, and some of them served on various boards of directors. It is hard to tell someone who

---

[39] Jelena Debeljak and Kristijan, "'Me, Myself, and I': Practical Egoism, Selfishness, Self-Interest and Business Ethics," *Social Responsibility Journal* (2008): 217.
[40] Maidique and Hiller, 77.
[41] Ibid.
[42] Ibid.,78.
[43] Ibid.
[44] Christopher Robertson and Scott Geiger, "Moral Philosophy and Managerial Perceptions of Ethics Codes," *Cross Cultural Management*, 355.

has a prominent position to be quiet and just listen; however, Linda's professor did not shy away from taking control of his class. Even though he was dealing with well-respected leaders, the professor let them know that in his class, they were leaders in the making. A few of the students decided to challenge the professor on every topic, forcing the professor to address the ongoing disruption: it had become an unwanted issue in the learning environment.

Linda noticed that the professor was becoming irritated at the students' continuous challenges. The professor presented the ground rules for future interactions. He started by thanking everyone for enrolling in his class, but he stressed in a stern tone that he was the leader in the class. He understood that Linda's classmates were leaders, but he told them to leave their ego at the door (LEAD) before joining his classroom. Carter says, "Egos refuse to let people see the error of their ways. There is nothing wrong with authority if it is properly channeled; the wrong power can cripple an organization."[45] The students apologized for their continuous interruptions. Maybe they realized that even their egos had limitations, especially in the course.

Chameleon Mindsets

Maidique and Hiller state,

> Leaders with a chameleon mindset are adaptive, they rarely reach the senior leadership level, but they can work their way up the organization by pleasing other people in power. Leaders with a chameleon mindset usually struggle with low self-esteem, always seeking a need to be

---

[45] Harry R. Carter, *Effective Leaders Check Their Egos at the Door* (Firehouse, 2006), 87.

> accepted by others. Leaders with a chameleon mindset lack courage and struggle with making a tough decision ... they are useful in participating in an organization's strategic project, but they will falter when opposition arose or presented with challenging questions about the project.[46]

They continue, "Leaders with a chameleon mindset usually select to serve people who are the most important to them on a given day. ... Leaders with a chameleon usually do not commit to specific values, portraying to others that they are spineless."[47] As a result, team members will not follow them during difficult times.[48] Leaders with a chameleon mindset will serve anyone.

However, Geedy notes, "the positive side to being a chameleon is to demonstrate a high capacity for adjustment."[49] She concedes, "Being a quick-change artist can build your reputation as a leader, and mobility makes you a valuable member of the leadership team in an ethical manner."[50] One of the most important things is to add value to the process of change.[51]

On the leadership journey, Linda can attest to working with a colleague having a chameleon mindset. The colleague was transitioning from an external organization into a higher leadership role. The colleague was excited to be part of an amazing team, and she made it openly known to her superiors. Linda made sure the colleague was comfortable in the new

---

[46] Maidique and Hiller, 78.
[47] Ibid.
[48] Ibid.
[49] Nancy M. Geedey, "Following a New Roadmap to Leadership Success," *Nursing Management* (2004): 49.
[50] Ibid.
[51] Ibid., 50.

surroundings. Yet, Linda noticed that the colleague began to demonstrate a "go with the flow" attitude about different issues among team members, showing a need to be accepted by them. Linda became suspicious of the colleague's behavior, and she began to observe additional interactions, noticing she had a chameleon's mindset.

Linda observed more chameleon behaviors in the colleague; she was being flexible in crisis situations, and her productivity seemed to increase around the superiors. Linda asked the colleague for help, but the colleague stated, "I really do not have the time. I am having lunch with a possible business partner." Linda realized the colleague was doing whatever it took to get herself ahead. The colleague had scheduled a time to meet with people of importance from her perspective, and Linda was not on the list. Linda noticed that the colleague was constantly adjusting her personality and availability according to people with the most influence within the organization. The colleague's behavior caused a trust issue among the members: she would commit to a project only if it meant being recognized and accepted by senior leaders. What would have happened if the colleague's approach was different? The team's synergy would have improved, and they would have trusted her more as a leader; they could have learned from her expertise.

Dynamo Mindset

Leaders with a dynamo mindset are strategic thinkers; "they help people persistently execute strategy."[52] Leaders with a dynamo mindset are shiners in their profession.[53] "Their colleagues depend on them," say Maidique and Hiller; "they exist on the junior and senior level within organizations."[54] However,

---

[52] Maidique and Hiller, 78.
[53] Ibid.
[54] Ibid.

"there is a weakness with a dynamo mindset, individuals can lose sight of the bigger picture in pursuit of achieving the objective."[55] Leaders with a dynamo mindset are usually not resistant to the words *change*, *future*, and *strategy*. They remain in the ready position to create plans that will ensure efficiency and effectiveness within organizations.

In fact, say Hopkins et al.,

> Managers at the top and middle levels of organizations have been associated with strategic renewal. The mindset of top management can directly influence middle managers perceptions of the empowerment they have to impact organizational current and future goals.[56]

They continue, saying, "Leaders with a dynamo mindset should have an understanding of environment dimensions and organizational priorities, be able to devise actions and create realistic estimates of the outcomes connected with those actions."[57] Leaders with a dynamo mindset create a strategy for optimal outcomes; they are foresight individuals.

Linda's boss called her to share the future plan for the organization. Linda was told that a merger would occur between her company and another organization. Linda was not surprised by the news; it had been a hot topic in previous years, brewing in conversation among company employees. Linda's boss was concerned about how the change would affect the team, since another company was involved. Linda was asked to create a strategy for the transitioning phase of the merger. To develop the strategy, Linda must understand

---

[55] Maidique and Hiller, 79.
[56] Willie E. Hopkins, Paul Mallette, and Shirley A. Hopkins, "Proposed Factors Influencing Strategic Inertial Strategic Renewal in Organizations," *Academy of Strategic Management Journal* (2013): 77.
[57] Ibid., 89.

"financial strength, market position, management strength and the overall health of the other company."[58]

When seeking that information, Linda was operating under an important mantra: "[Linda] was aware that those aspects that might be considered cultural were extremely vital for the merger."[59] In fact, she was cognizant of "the style of the company, its technological origins, its structure, and its ways of operating, all of which might provide clues as to its basic assumptions about its mission and its future."[60] Linda had to know about the other company's organizational culture before the merger occurred to prevent a clash of cultures. This required a number of steps.

Step 1. Linda utilized the following strategy for change starting with culture:

> Leaders must understand their own organizational culture well enough to be able to sense if there are hidden issues which could clash with another organizational culture. Leaders must be able to influence the other culture to engage in activities that will reveal to them and to the other organization what some of its assumptions are. Leaders must be able to discern and present the incompatibilities in a manner for those involved in the decision-making process can understand and adjust to the cultural realities. Leaders that are not in a senior position must be able to influence the senior leaders of the importance and severity of cultural issues.[61]

---

[58] Edgard H. Schein, *Organizational Culture and Leadership*, (Jossey-Bass, 2010), 377.
[59] Ibid.
[60] Ibid.
[61] Ibid., 379.

Step 2. Leaders need to effectively communicate the overall strategic plan, vision, and mission, being transparent about answering difficult questions, remembering to reduce the rumor mill.

Step 3. Leaders need to meet with all people involved as individuals and collectively, providing in-depth information about the future condition of the merger. Leaders need to schedule routine meetings until the merger has occurred.

Step 4. Leaders need to refrain from getting caught up in the "political process" and stay focus on becoming one culture.[62] They need to restate the mission and organizational objectives for clarity.

Step 5. Leaders need to be accessible for employees during the transition, providing different modes for accessibility and communication. Employees should be able to ask questions in a timely manner and receive a timely response.

Linda's actions demonstrated a dynamo mindset by ensuring the strategy was implemented and executed according to her boss's request. The two merging organizational cultures became one culture with minimum opposition. Having a strategic mindset was the key factor in accomplishing the desired goals.

Builder Mindset

Leaders with a builder mindset usually are centered on the organization as a whole.[63] They are long-term thinkers and foresight thinkers.[64] Maidique and Hiller note, "Leaders with a builder mindset exist on different levels, not only as senior leaders."[65] The organization is a combination of multiple units

---

[62] Ibid.
[63] Maidique and Hiller, 79.
[64] Ibid.
[65] Ibid.

working collaboratively together as one unit.[66] "No matter what the role is," Maidique and Hiller say, "everyone can work together, building an organization that carries out a broader vision."[67] They add, "Leaders with a builder mindset serve the institution,"[68] wanting the best for its present and future state.

In fact, an organization's leaders must be mindful of its culture hindsight, insight, and foresight to be innovative and produce growth, which can lead to success. Hindsight is viewing the past occurrences, insight is viewing into an occurrence, and foresight is getting prepared for future occurrences; all three of them are interrelated for decision-making and the building process. It has been said, "Hindsight is a wonderful thing, but predicting what hindsight might tell you is even better. It allows the organization to discover possible issues sooner than later based on past experiences, preventing repeatable problems."[69]

Having a builder's mindset often requires organizational guidelines for new staff. When Linda started her career as an employee, she was required to take courses that supported the organization as a whole. The courses were directly related to the organization's beliefs and values, and they were provided and taught by leaders within the organization. Linda recalled sitting in the classroom while a young man provided a presentation on values. She was amazed at the presenter's passion for the organization and its core values. "Wow!" Linda commented. He clearly loved his profession. Linda thought maybe the presenter was stretching the truth about the organization's values, though. She asked, "Are there organizations that truly believe in executing excellence in service?" As Linda continued to listen, she wanted to hear more about working

---

[66] Ibid.
[67] Ibid.
[68] Ibid.
[69] Anonymous, "Why Product Managers Don't Cry Over Spilt Milk," *Strategic Direction* (2004): 22.

with an excellent attitude, being an employee with integrity, and using each opportunity for the best. In addition, her personal values were similar to the organization's values.

Therefore, Linda decided to speak with the presenter after the course. She waited in line until it was her turn. She had a brief discussion about values, in other words, serving the organization as a whole. She felt as if the interaction was a divine moment in her work life, without knowledge of the future. She enjoyed meeting someone who believed in the institution's values. Linda left the session feeling empowered to be an employee working for the best company. Later, she found out that the presenter served both internally and externally within the organization as a leader with a builder mindset. Ultimately, the presenter became Linda's mentor and changed her perspective on leading others through vision, foresight, and building herself for the organization.

Transcender Mindset

Maidique and Hiller state, "Leaders with a transcender mindset are broad thinkers. ... Leaders with a transcender mindset often try to maximize the value for shareholders, both internally and externally, from their current position."[70] Sonneberg adds, "People should be encouraged to become broad thinkers and not have tunnel vision. They are good at managing in complex situations, understanding how all of the pieces fit as a whole."[71] Leaders with a transcender mindset feel socially responsible for the community. They are often committed to performing community service, utilizing their voice to make improvements for the good of mankind.

For instance, Linda often felt socially responsible for her

---

[70] Maidique and Hiller, 79.
[71] Frank K. Sonnenberg, "Cultivating Creativity," *Executive Excellence* (1991): 13.

community. She decided to return to her childhood neighborhood to help with their needs. Linda began a partnership with the complex management team to support their back-to-school drive for school children. Linda, her family, and her friends donate school supplies and their time to ensure middle and high school children had supplies according the requirements. During the event, Linda spent hours talking to both parents and children about life and their future, reminding them to keep pushing forward to better things in life.

Summary: Building Block Two

Being an effective leader requires having a leadership mindset, another part of the strategy. What is a leadership mindset? It can influence the decision-making process and stance of a leader. There are different leadership mindsets within organizations—some with negative characteristics, such as sociopath and egoist, and some with positive characteristics, such as dynamo, builder, and transcender mindsets, and some with both negative and positive characteristics, such as chameleon. All of them can influence an organization's culture, direction, and financial performance. Leadership thinking is crucial for the overall value for leaders and organizations.

Chapter 3

Leadership Development: Mentoring, Coaching, and Consulting

Leadership Development

Are individuals born as leaders, or do they develop as leaders? This is a question that has puzzled scholars for years. According to Gartner, "The best answer to this question is, no one knows for sure."[72] When it comes to leadership, there are so many different perspectives, opinions, and standpoints. Gartner adds that leaders appear to develop and act differently according to their chosen field—a factor that only increases speculation about leadership development.[73] He notes, "Leadership is determined by a combination of many traits and behaviors, not just one, nor is there only one area for individuals to exhibit leadership qualities."[74]

---

[72] Tony Gartner, "Commentary: Leaders Are Born, Not Made, or Are They," *St. Charles County Business Record* (2004): 1.
[73] Ibid.
[74] Ibid.

However, strong leaders do exhibit similar characteristics that add to their success, namely specialized knowledge, a developed moral compass, selflessness, communicating well-formed goals to their followers, and a bright outlook on life.[75] Strong leaders are supportive of their employees, they are visible, and they are accessible, and these types of leaders set the best example for followership.[76] Arshavski insists, "Whether born or made, there are traits and qualities that it takes to become an effective leader."[77] Yet, some leadership characteristics seem in an individual's life can be a direct result of his or her upbringing and surroundings. In fact, "the ability to see way into the future, gives good leaders a distinctive insight into what they need to do now, in order to accomplish that future which in turns highlights the essence of leadership."[78]

As a teenager, Linda was excited about her future life. She felt as if she was born as a leader, needing more leadership development. Linda had several leadership characteristics before becoming an adult such as utilizing her moral compass, selflessness; she had a bright outlook on life. She was a quiet person with bigger-than-life goals and dreams. Linda had a sense of ethics in her relationships, making sure she treated others fairly with an expectation of being treated in the same manner. Linda enjoyed high school; she was often the leader in her inner group, making sure everyone went to school and performed well in their coursework. Linda discouraged her graduating friends from skipping class on "Senior Skip Day"— she was frowned upon by others for this choice, but Linda was not offended by their comments as she went to class.

Accordingly, Linda had a passion for school, especially in her Health Service Aide (HSA) course. Linda had learned about

---

[75] Olson, 30.
[76] Ibid.
[77] Marina Arshavski, "Great Leadership," *Leadership Excellence Essentials* (2016): 10.
[78] Ibid., 11.

the body systems and their functions in her junior year of high school, and the HSA class was taught by a registered nurse who wore a white uniform with a nursing cap. The HSA course was a two-year program with a clinical rotation in the second year at a local hospital. Linda had the opportunity to provide direct patient care through feeding, taking vitals, bathing, transporting, and assisting patients.

The clinicals were rewarding for Linda and her classmates. They would work together, performing all the responsibilities assigned to them by the nursing leadership. Linda and her classmates would compete in distributing ice and water to all the patients, starting on the opposite side of the hospital hallway and moving swiftly as the nursing staff would smile and observe. Linda felt appreciated, and it was at that time she decided to become a charge nurse. She had observed healthcare as compassionate care, and she was comfortable working and leading in a healthcare setting, always helping her classmates. At the end of Linda's clinical rotation, the nursing staff provided an appreciation lunch for the class. Linda and her classmates received a card from the nursing staff that read, "Our thanks for all your help and continued success in all you do!" The card contained signatures from the nursing leadership and staff. Linda realized that she had made a real difference in a professional healthcare organization as a teenager.

Succeeding in the coursework was not enough for Linda as a teenager; she wanted to do more in her community. Some of the teenagers around Linda were getting in trouble, hanging around the wrong type of people and wasting time. Linda had met a woman whose children needed help with their coursework. Linda agreed to tutor the children for free in the evening time. As a result of the relationship, the woman—who took on an overseeing role—and Linda developed a youth program for their community. It was called "The Junior Express Club." The purpose of the program was to provide the teenagers with life skills and knowledge to use as they transitioned into adulthood, and Linda and her overseer received sponsorship from a local city councilman, businessmen, women, and the parents and guardians of the members.

In a well-orchestrated display of youth responsibility, all the program's leadership positions were occupied by teenagers. Linda was the vice president of the program; she had to support the president in his absences, along with other tasks. The program had about thirteen members who attended the same high school. The members were exposed to banking courses and other seminars held at a local college, as well as lectures from community leaders. Through the program, Linda as a teenager had learned about trust and the overall commitment of a leader. In fact, the mentoring and coaching that Linda was introduced to in the program had prepared and developed her for the future leadership roles. During the existence of the program, the overseer provided feedback to the members and their parents, ensuring they were heading on the right path in life for adulthood.

Just as Linda and her fellow leaders were sponsored and supported by older adults, there are practices to support individuals' leadership while they support others in their roles. To develop their leadership, individuals can utilize mentoring, coaching, consulting, and education as a means to enhance their leadership style. Growth and development are crucial for individuals' effectiveness as leaders, and learning is an ongoing process in which leaders must invest in themselves as well as others.

Mentoring

In a passionate assertion of the importance of mentoring, Wlesh et al. explain, "If individuals are going to be a success in the workplace, they need a mentor for development and improvement."[79] Mentoring is about shaping another individual's life through counseling or guidance. It involves taking a special interest in someone and spiritually or professionally developing them.[80] Garvey asserts, "Mentoring is a natural activity of human life-cycle, and it is beneficial to the individuals and the organization by reducing stress, less absenteeism, and improving learning."[81] In fact, it can have a lasting impression on individuals.[82] Mentoring indicates the value of an employee,[83] and investing in that employee can improve overall organizational culture.

The mentoring relationship consists of a mentor (the person counseling or teaching another person in the relationship) and the mentee (the person being advised, guided, or counseled in the relationship). Mentoring is further divided into sponsorship and development. Sponsorship mentoring places the relationship's power in the wealth and influence of the mentor—an increasingly unpopular form of training leaders.[84] "With developmental mentoring," on the other hand, "the focus is on the support of learning, and the importance of helping mentees do things for themselves, empowering them."[85] In opposition to sponsorship, developmental mentoring works to improve the mentee through mental improvement.[86] In developmental mentoring, the mentor can

---

[79] Elizabeth Torney Wlesh, Devasheesh Bhave, and Kyoung Young Kim, "Are You My Mentor? Informal Mentoring Mutual Identification," *Career Development International* (2012): 137.

[80] Stephen Gibb, "Evaluating Mentoring," *Education & Training* (1994): 32.

[81] Bob Garvey, "First-Person Mentoring," *Career Development International* (1996): 10.

[82] Ibid.

[83] Ibid.

[84] David Clutterbuck, "What's Happening in Coaching and Mentoring? And What Is the Difference between Them?" *Development and Learning in Organizations* (2008): 8.

[85] Ibid.

[86] Ibid.

establish objectives for the mentee to accomplish over a short or long period.[87]

Mentor's Characteristics

However, the mentor needs to have precise qualities in place for the experience to be prosperous for the mentee. Dean reminds scholars, "The mentor serves as sounding boards for mentees."[88] This was seen with Linda. She met with her mentor after having a bad day. Linda told her mentor about the frustrations that she had experienced, and he didn't judge her, but he listened to her. He allowed Linda to have real feelings and emotions even if she had a wrong perspective. The mentoring relationship is stronger when a "mentor is a good listener" during the sessions.[89] As a result, "some elements are seen such as consistent eye contact, each person is facing each other during the conversation, each person is waiting until the person speaking is finished," allowing the mentee time to express his or her feeling or thoughts.[90] A mentor must also understand and respect their mentee's emotions and proceed accordingly.[91] This dialogue of understanding "will develop room for openness and acceptance, demonstrating that the mentor is in-tune with the mentee's ambitions."[92] Linda's mentor created an atmosphere in which Linda was open and honest about her present and future work life.

Dean also notes, "Good mentors give attention to increasing the mentee's capacity for more responsibility and

---

[87] Ibid.
[88] Peter J. Dean, "Nine Traits to Look for in a Mentor," *Agent Sales Journal* (2006).
[89] Ibid.
[90] Ibid.
[91] Ibid.
[92] Ibid.

higher-level work."[93] Effective mentors are problem-solvers, looking for opportunities to making the flow of things more smoothly.[94] They normally hold themselves to a personally high code o ethics, enabling them to guide their mentee in moral as well as vocational situations.[95] However, if an individual shows any signs of egoism, that person should not be considered for a mentor role. "A society made up of ethical egoists," says Dean, "would be dominated by opportunistic behavior which can lead to actions that bring harm to others"[96] Good mentors always respond to negative situations respectfully[97] and are great communicators. "They usually speak with specificity," adds Dean.[98] Spending time with a good mentor will sharpen an individual's personal and professional life over time. As a result of Linda's time with her mentor, she went from having a diploma in respiratory therapy to obtaining a doctorate degree in strategic leadership. Linda understands the importance of having a good mentor.

Developing a Mentoring Program

Therefore, if organizations lack mentoring, they need to create a mentorship program that fosters a learning environment. The leaders of organizations without such programs need a step-by-step strategy for their mentorship development.

1. The organization's leadership team needs to perform an internal assessment of its current culture state, looking for baseline data on the need for a mentorship program.

---

[93] Ibid.
[94] Ibid.
[95] Ibid.
[96] Ibid.
[97] Ibid.
[98] Ibid.

2. The organization must develop an assessment to gain information concerning the needs of existing employees.[99]
3. Before implementation, the organization's leadership team must have a clear understanding of mentoring to collect useful data.[100]
4. The questions leadership asks employees should be centered on the question: "Why do you want a mentoring program?"[101]
5. Based on the returned data, the organization's leadership team should "plan and design the mentoring program."[102]
6. The organization's leadership team should "create participants' training" sessions, online modules, and other learning avenues for employees.[103]
7. A small test of change should occur, "using a pilot program" such as a small group of leaders and employees.[104]
8. Once the pilot program has been used for some time, it needs to be evaluated for its effectiveness.[105] Any evaluations developed for potential mentees must be measured against the organization's vision.[106] Rolfe notes that upper executives and stakeholders in an organization may have their own ideas of good mentorship.[107] "This is why," he expounds, "input and feedback is a

---

[99] Allan H. Church and Janine Waclawski, *Designing and Using Organizational Surveys: A Seven-Step Process*, (Jossey-Bass, 2001), 4.
[100] Ann Rolfe, "How to Design Your Mentoring Program," *Training and Development in Australia* (2008): 32.
[101] Ibid.
[102] Ibid.
[103] Ibid.
[104] Ibid.
[105] Ibid.
[106] Rolfe, 34.
[107] Ibid.

requirement in the initial phase. The evaluation is likely to include another instrument with simple questions and a rating scale."[108]
9. Based on the results from the pilot program's evaluation, the leadership team should look for adjustments and other "components to be used in the new mentoring program."[109]
10. The final phase is to roll out the mentoring program throughout the organization with checkpoints every six months.

Linda as a Mentee

Linda's mentor agreed to support her. He had heard about her professional and compassionate reputation from other team members in the organization. The mentor had provided Linda with a look into his leadership track from the past to his current position. The mentoring relationship came at a time when her career had stagnated. Linda wanted another challenge in her work life, but she had limited exposure within the organization. During the first meeting with her mentor, Linda was asked about higher education and if she would consider going back to school. Linda was a little hesitant since she had been out of school for a while. Eventually, though, Linda listened to her mentor's advice and decided to seek a bachelor's degree in leadership.

The mentor met with Linda at least once a month for a progress report; although he was busy with his leadership assignments, he always scheduled a time to listen and give Linda recommendations. The mentor was a highly effective leader who was well respected throughout the organization. Linda made sure she was prepared for sessions with her mentor,

---
[108] Ibid.
[109]

since she did not want to waste his time. The mentor always left Linda with assignments to perform before their next session. Linda was given the assignment of meeting with other leaders within the organization. Linda was given the assignment of taking courses for professional development. Linda was assigned to an external committee for the organization. Linda did not want to disappoint her mentor, so she made sure she was making some progress in her personal and work life.

Linda admired the mentor's leadership style. He made leadership seem easy and interesting and was a transformational leader. Tucker and Russell argue, "It is an individual who creates an inspiring vision, facilitates the vision, encourages short-term sacrifices, and makes pursuing the vision a fulfilling event." Linda's mentor appeared to be just that type of inspiring individual.[110] Truly motivating leaders, Tucker and Russell continue, are adept at motivating others by encouraging them to catch the leader's vision for growth.[111] "Transformational leaders concentrate on change, progress, and development," they add.[112] Linda had never witnessed her mentor upset about anything—he remained calm and even-toned in his speech. However, Linda still struggled with understanding unethical leadership skills. She could not understand why her direct boss behaved in ways opposite to the organization's core values. The mentor advised Linda to take a different perspective on leadership and look at things from another view, almost like a textbook answer. In fact, "transformational leaders desire to influence the way people think and introduce new processes into the organization."[113] Linda wanted to complain about his suggestions concerning her boss's behavior, but the mentor

---

[110] Bruce A. Tucker and Robert F. Russell, "The Influence of the Transformational Leader," *Journal of Leadership and Organizational Studies* (2004): 103.
[111] Ibid.
[112] Ibid., 105.
[113] Ibid.

found a way to redirect any negative energy: he set expectations and projected outcomes for each session.

Linda's mentor introduced her to serving the community through leadership in an established organization. She was allowed to serve on a committee with an external organization to support people with health-related issues. Linda continued with higher education, pursuing a master's degree in leadership. The mentor made sure that Linda was recognized for her progress as a leader through direct feedback and emails to others. Linda realized that she had a strong mentor; he changed her mindset and behavior as an employee and leader.

- ☐ Linda had become more optimistic.
- ☐ Linda had become more motivated.
- ☐ Linda concentrated on the bigger picture.
- ☐ Linda had become more goal and outcome oriented.

Linda as a Mentor

Linda can recall the moment she was first asked to be an official mentor, after working for the organization more than twenty-five years. She was serving in a leadership role as a supervisor. Another leader within the organization made the request. Linda's mentee was a gentleman from a different cultural background and a different work area—differences that were important for Linda to understand. Cultural understanding affects every area that mentors attempt to improve in their mentees: communication, leadership skills, and vulnerability.[114] In fact, "developing cultural agility requires active engagement in knowledge acquisition, experiential learning, and personal reflection."[115] Linda had to learn about the personal

---

[114] Paula Caliqiuri, "Develop Your Cultural Agility," *Training and Development* (2013): 70.
[115] Ibid., 71.

and leadership values of her mentee's culture through research and having a personal discussion with the mentee. She met with her mentee every two weeks in the beginning, then once a month as time moved forward. Linda ensured that the mentee had both personal and professional short- and long-term objectives, created by him and adjusted by her, as they worked together in the mentorship. Goals—another important aspect of the mentor-mentee relationship—should be set and approved by both parties.[116]

However, the mentee experienced an issue with an employee under his leadership that threatened his balance between authority and empathy. The mentee was extremely tough in mandating an attendance policy; the employee under him was dealing with a personal matter that caused her to be late at times. Linda asked the mentee if there were any other options to support the employee without penalizing her, so the mentee decided to look for another option to help the employee by the suggesting Employee Assistance Program (EAP).

For some employees, it is difficult to leave their personal problems at the entrance of an organization before working, and it hurts for a leader to ignore them. Steiber reminds employers that "if it were possible for employees to separate their personal problems from their work, or for an employee to ensure that productivity was unaffected by personal issues, there would be no need for organizations to provide an EAP."[117] Leaders need to understand the whole person, both work life and home life. Linda was teaching the mentee to find the root of the problem and address it by being supportive. "In the past," Steiber says, "EAP experts often estimated that 20

---

[116] Julie Todaro, "Mentoring: Advice from an Expert," *Library Leadership and Management Online* (2011): 2.
[117] Gus Stieber, "A Rx for Problems Affecting Job Performance: EAPs," *ACA News* (1999): 41.

percent of any workforce was impacted by personal problems that have an effect on job performance."[118]

Sometimes, individuals become an influence in someone else's life without an introduction as an official mentor; it just happens. Linda met a college student who was seeking a degree in journalism, and as their relationship developed, the student often called Linda for advice on educational decisions. The student wanted to know if she should drop out of college and work a fulltime job. Linda, in response, advised the student to write down all the pros and cons of each situation and make a decision. The student decided to decrease her class load and work a part-time job to balance her goals. As a result of the student's continued progress, she was selected to write an article for the college's newsletter. The student also participated in seminars hosted by the news broadcast staff, and when asked if she had a mentor, the student told them about Linda, even though mentorship was never bluntly discussed between them. Linda was proud to have been considered a mentor.

Coaching

Mentoring and coaching are related. While mentoring is instilling something into individuals, coaching is pulling something already present out from individuals and developing them to their best potential. It is a practice that leaves those coached with greater skills and wisdom and opens doors to use the tools they develop under their coach.[119] "Leadership coaching," to specify further, "is a one-on-one partnership that focuses on strengthening the self-efficacy and performance of the individual, and consequently,

---

[118] Ibid., 42.
[119] Liske Reyes, Jessica M., and Courtney L. Holladay, "Evaluating Coaching's Effect: Competencies, Career Mobility and Retention," *Leadership and Organizational Development Journal* (2016): 937.

improving organizational effectiveness."[120] Leadership coaching aims to improve individuals' leadership skills, decision-making, and overall leadership behaviors that will help their organizations to be more successful, which eventually gives organizations a competitive advantage in their industry.[121] Some organizations provide coaching as a means for ongoing leaders' and followers' development.[122] Still, "in order to be successful in coaching, organizations can create a culture where leaders can adopt coaching skills as the way to lead others."[123] Coaching is a learned skill, and individuals can improve in their coaching capacity even as they encourage those under them to coach.[124]

Coaching offers creative methods for employees to become their best through "talent development."[125] Coaching allows leaders to ask questions, thus empowering employees and bringing out the best in them.[126] It requires a commitment from all parties involved: "the upfront investment can produce long-term benefits."[127] Coaching helps leaders encourage those under them to take the risks in work and life, and studies on effective coaching prove it increases the effectiveness of teams.[128] Overall, coaching can improve employees' "motivation and organizational culture" for the better.[129]

---

[120] Erica Anthony, "The Impact of Leadership Coaching on Leadership Behaviors," *The Journal of Management Development* (2017): 930.
[121] Ibid.
[122] Jack Zenger and Kathleen Stinnett, "Why Coach?" *Leadership Excellence* (2007): 20.
[123] Ibid.
[124] Ibid.
[125] Weblog Post, "Leadership Freak: Stop Pushing—Create Pull," *Newstex Global Business Blogs* (2015).
[126] Ibid.
[127] Ibid.
[128] Mike McDermott, Alec Levenson, and Suzanne Newton, "What Coaching Can and Cannot Do for Your Organization," *HR. Human Resource Planning* (2007): 30.
[129] Ibid.

Senger and Stinnett note, "When leaders are acting as a coach, they can provide guidance to help others perform, grow and develop."[130] One of Linda's employees was having difficulty working with others, a huge deficiency in the teamwork of the organization. He had been with the organization for many years, and he wanted things to remain the same throughout any changes. The employee had become complacent in the setting, and it was reflected in his routine: Upon coming to work, he would not take a patient report from anyone on the ongoing staff unless he had all of his personal belongings in alignment with his workspace, causing others to wait for him. The other team members would comment about the situation among themselves until it became a breaking point for them. Once, the situation became a shouting match between the employee and his team members. Afterward, the team members brought the problem to Linda. She had to research the situation, getting information from everyone who had witnessed the encounter. Linda discovered that other issues were surrounding the same employee. Other departments were complaining about the lack of teamwork, and he appeared to be disrespectful when interacting with other people.

The employee wanted to complete all his work in a timely fashion without any interruption. However, it did not always work out in that manner; unexpected calls for patient care would arise as part of the employee's assignments, and although time was allotted for the interruptions, the employee preferred a single track of progression in his day-to-day work. Linda had to meet with the employee, since his behavior was not adhering to the company's values and his stubbornness was causing discomfort for others in the organization's culture. Outside the workplace, the employee was nevertheless known to provide assistance for others in his family and community, making sure others' needs were being met. He often hosted

---

[130] Zenger and Stinnett, 20.

gatherings for everyone to assemble during the holidays; he enjoyed the fellowship. He was also dependable, always working scheduled shifts and keeping his time.

Nevertheless, there appeared to be a problem: something was causing a behavioral change in the employee; the employee had began to yell and become impatient with others. Linda met with the employee, and she told him about the concerns regarding the changes in his behavior in addition to addressing his lack of teamwork. The employee admitted to feeling different, but he had not realized that others noticed. He was trying to manage his tasks on his own, keeping frustrations to a minimum, but it was getting harder. Linda offered to help the employee, and he agreed to accept the support. Linda created a coaching strategy for the employee. As Hawkins says, "It is a fact that coaching has three clients: the individual; the organization; and the relationship between the two."[131]

Coaching Strategy

Linda developed her coaching strategy by working backward, starting with the goals she wanted the employee to achieve and setting up steps to reach them.[132] For instance, with the employee who had teamwork issues, Linda provided the goal and steps.

- ☐ Goal: to enhance teamwork among others.
- ☐ Steps: (1) come to work prepared with a good attitude (2) start work in a timely manner (3) use time wisely (4) complete work in excellence (5) assist others once work is completed.

---

[131] Peter Hawkins, "Developing an Effective Coaching Strategy," *Global Focus* (2009): 15.
[132] Ibid.

She added resources, such as EAP, to make the coaching appear nonthreatening and to use what she had available to her as a leader.[133] She devloped her company's coaching strategy more by paying attention to the way that coaching behaviors eventually affected employees' interaction with teams and organizational situations.[134] Linda implemented the coaching strategy, and the employee's behavior changed positively. The employee's colleagues began to recognize his contribution to teamwork.

Consulting

Another part to enhancing leadership development is consulting. It differs from mentoring (telling others) and coaching (drawing out in others). Dyck defines this as "the art of influencing people at their request."[135] "Consulting," she says, " is reaching a conclusion of acceptable quality, maintaining an acceptable commitment to that conclusion, and supporting the client to prevent or minimize any detrimental outcomes as a result of the conclusion."[136] Consulting options can be obtained from internal or external sources, depending on an organization's needs. It requires an individual to "know their own motivation, attitudes, and aptitude" if they are expecting to become an expert in the field.[137] "Consulting can be tremendous fun," adds McKnight.[138] He notes that consultants are uniquely positioned to learn about their clients' needs,

---

[133] Ibid.
[134] Ibid., 17.
[135] Dianne Dyck, "Internal and External Consulting: Assisting Clients with Managing Work, Health, and Psychosocial Issues," *AAOHN Journal* (2002): 111.
[136] Ibid.
[137] Carol Harris, "Consulting and You," *Consulting to Management* (2001): 49.
[138] William McKnight, *90 Days to Success in Consulting* (Cengage Learning, 2010), 19.

more so than even the clients themselves. Consultants perform a variety of marketing and communication tasks as they work to grow their clients' potential.[139] They must continuously network and "be self-motivated and self-promoted."[140] Just like leadership, coaching, or mentoring, " consulting is a personal relationship."[141] Consultants understand that, oftentimes, their clients need help with navigating interpersonal communication instead of growing in vocational knowledge.[142] Consultants usually involves providing an assessment of the organization with recommendations for improvement, or identifying areas of opportunity through a professional consulting report.

Consulting Report

As part of the consulting process, leadership development can be strengthened.

On consulting, Bendall argues, "One of the most tangible things that an organization can receive from consultants is the suitability report."[143] However, a consulting report may vary depending on the type of firm it studies. Overall, "it gives a detailed summary of where they are, where they are trying to move toward, and how they will get there with using a consulting firm."[144] The consulting report should be professionally formatted in a "brief and simple" outline, since most clients want consultants to find answer to problems quickly and without much burden.[145] Consulting experts remind readers that

---

[139] Ibid.
[140] Anonymous, "Should You Be a Consultant? 6 Tips to Help You Decide," *Training* (1997): S8.
[141] McKnight., 93.
[142] Ibid.
[143] Kim Bendall, "The Seven Basic Principles Of Client Report Writing," *Professional Adviser* (2014): 16.
[144] Ibid.
[145] Ibid.

consulting reports should capture audiences and remain easy to digest, containing plain language, diagrams when needed, and appendices for dense and detailed information.[146] "The main body of the report should contain the recommendations, costs, and charges," says Bendall.[147] A standard report should also have some of the following components:

- ☐ Table of contents
- ☐ Confidential statement
- ☐ Letter to leadership
- ☐ Executive summary
- ☐ The scope of the report
- ☐ Methodology
- ☐ Recommendations
- ☐ Closing findings
- ☐ Bibliography
- ☐ Biography of the consultant
- ☐ Contact information

The consultant compiling the report should share it with their client as a presentation, preparing ahead of time for an informative discussion about the health of the organization and how specifically to meet the needs of their client. Consulting is about making a difference in the lives of organizations, building new relationships, and strengthening old ones in the process.

Linda's Sample Report

Linda was pursuing higher education with consulting as a concentration but decided to change her course. She had basic consulting experience throughout the workplace. However,

---

[146] Ibid.
[147] Ibid.

Linda decided to use the consulting knowledge that was presented to her in an educational leadership program. Linda wanted to utilize some of the information to acquire practice in the field, just to see if she could properly assess an organization. Linda wanted to offer any organization a free assessment with no obligations, and though she was inexperienced, she considered herself ready for the challenge.

Linda was required to travel once a year as part of higher education. She enjoyed flying, but she did not appreciate traveling through big airports, requiring her to run from point A to point B within a few minutes. Linda's last trip was a scary experience, as she got lost in midst of moving around, and it produced panic and fear, but she tried to make the trip a pleasant experience. She tried to avoid traveling through a specific airport, but she could not get around it. Linda decided to give it a chance, but she felt a little worried and highly overwhelmed in the second airport, which was chaotic. Linda had to take two flights, in both directions, before reaching her destination. Linda decided to take a different approach on the returning flights: she decided to overcome the fear and anxiety with assessing the situation, which led to Linda writing a simple consulting report free of charge for the airport. Linda decided to send a certified copy to the airport's leadership team, hoping to make a small difference in other customers' travel experiences. Linda's report is transcribed in the appendix of this book. Months later, Linda found herself traveling through the same airport, and it was the best experience. The signage reflected where Linda was located and where she was headed. The changes that Linda suggested were present. Linda provided recommendations for better service, and it was evident that something had changed.

Summary: Building Block Three

Leaders need tools and practices to support their leadership style, prompting them to become better leaders while improving others. Leadership development positions individuals for successful outcomes in their personal and work life. Leaders are developed through mentoring, coaching, and consulting. Mentoring is an interactive process between a mentor and mentee, and it requires equal input from the mentee for the decision-making process. Mentoring means changing a person's life through influence and guidance. Coaching is changing a person's life by pulling out something within them, driving them to their best potential. Mentoring and coaching are connected, and both can be used together. Organizations should invest in their employees by creating a mentoring program. Also, leaders must create a strategy for coaching others. Consulting creates opportunities for leaders to serve others in a time of need, usually through a request for services. Consulting is usually done by an instrument assessment and concluded with a consulting report. It gives leaders a chance to make observations of a situation and provide recommendations for areas of strengthens and opportunities.

Chapter 4

Leadership Effectiveness

Leaders play an important role in their success. "Leaders are only good as their talents and their teams."[148] In turbulent times, "organizations must invest in leadership programs that will enhance leadership effectiveness." [149] Leaders can enjoy a degree of success within the process. However, the amount of success is truly dependent on the leader's willingness to become effective. " Leadership effectiveness concentrates largely on output measurability and accomplishment of shared goals."[150] Leadership effectiveness can be viewed as adjusting to variations in circumstance while developing and maintaining healthy working relationships.[151]

Yet, "there is something to be said about an individual's

---

[148] Erin Harrison, "Executive Leadership: Aligning Passion and Purpose," *Inside Counsel* (2013).
[149] Francis Amagoh, "Leadership Development and Leadership Effectiveness," *Management Decision* (2009): 989.
[150] Kiran Sakkar Sudha, M. G. Shanawaz, and Anam Farhat, "Leadership Styles, Leader's Effectiveness and Well-Being: Exploring Collective Efficacy as a Mediator," *Vision* (2016): 113.
[151] Ibid.

leadership style, and how it does impact leadership effectiveness."[152] "Organizations need the right kind of leadership to have a competitive advantage and survive." [153] In fact, "when leaders are effective, they are more innovative, creative with issues, welcome change and challenges, and usually increase in job performance."[154] A lack of effective leadership can place an organization at risk.[155]

"It can have an impact on the ability of organizations to create, implement and sustain its strategic plan."[156]

Therefore, leadership effectiveness is a continuous progression. Linda recalled taking several courses at the local community college as she was moving toward her decided future. Linda had a total of four courses, and Dr. Hightower was the professor in two of them. As Linda entered the first class on her first day (Psychology), she met a distinguished-looking man. He introduced himself by emphasizing his eight different degrees and his ability to write with both hands. Linda was astonished by his accomplishments, but she had a feeling that he would be a challenging professor. At the end of the class, while she was departing for a break, Linda decided to leave her books on the desk since she had to return there for the next class, Human Growth and Development. Linda had enjoyed the previous class, and she was looking forward to the next session.

As Linda entered the room, she heard a statement: "Sweetheart, you need to drop one of my classes, since you are not going to be able to pass both of them at the same time."[157] Linda was totally shocked at the professor's pleasant

---

[152] Ibid.
[153] Amagoh, 989.
[154] Ibid.
[155] Ibid., 990.
[156] Ibid.
[157] Howard J. Hightower, Psychology at Florida Community College of Jacksonville, 1983.

tone. He told the class about how students had struggled with his class. Linda thought about how the professor did not know her personal drive in life. How could he make an assumption without knowing her? Linda decided to drop the two other courses, and she kept his two courses.

However, the race had begun to unfold in both classes. The professor issued the same amount of work in both courses, a midterm which was nineteen pages, a final exam that was twenty-one pages, and a thirty-page workbook, too much work for a student. Linda was determined to prove that the professor's comments were wrong. After all, even though he had eight degrees, Linda could achieve the same thing if she applied herself. Linda had to have a plan in order to pass Hightower's courses. She went to the library every day for numerous hours to study both subjects, traveled with her books, and studied whenever she had a moment. Linda made cassette tapes with the class information on them, listening to them while doing other things. She had developed a desire to learn, a routine, and the determination to succeed in both courses. Linda turned in assignments, and they were returned with red and green markings saying, "You are what you produced." Dr. Hightower held a pen in each hand, writing each letter in a different color. Dr. Hightower's grading scale went as high as 5.0 and as low as 0.0. He had a different perspective on education. He was a brilliant man. Linda wanted to succeed, so she made sure her efforts were reflected in the work. She had become consumed with getting a positive outcome.

In the end, Hightower telling Linda that she could not perform a task in a certain manner stimulated Linda's confidence, pushing her to change the professor's perspective, and set a record in his courses, leaving a legacy. Linda was efficacious and finished both courses well; in fact, Dr. Hightower recognized Linda's effort in front of the entire class. "Sweetheart, you are the first person to receive two A's in both of my classes."[158] Linda was grateful; she felt as if she could do anything if she was focused and unwavering. Linda carried that professor's comments throughout her life. As an emerging leader, Linda was told by her psychology professor, Dr. J. Hightower (1983), "You are what you produced." She knew that her leadership effectiveness was a reflection of her personal and work life: a life filled with purpose, passion, and persistence.

Purpose

Purpose leads to leadership effectiveness in organizations. "The secret of success is steadiness of purpose."[159] It can move teams from a crisis moment to an impactful moment.[160] "Purpose is the bridge of authentic leadership."[161] Everyone has a purpose in life, but many people do not actually discover their purpose. " The research shows that a sense of purpose is created throughout life's journey and encompasses an individual's personal values, goals, and identity."[162] As a result, "the leader can see meaning in their purpose which often comes from having conquered many trials and tribulations and being influenced by significant others in their life and career to date."[163] A leader with purpose thinks and behaves differently, always making decisions for a meaningful end result. "A leader with purpose defines success in terms of the legacy they will leave."[164] "A Leader with a purpose understands the impact they intend to make in achieving both financial and

---

[158] Hightower, 1983.
[159] Kevin Cashman, "Purpose Principle," *Leadership Excellence* (2010): 7.
[160] Ibid.
[161] Ibid.
[162] Chris Underwood, "Purpose in Leadership," *Training Journal* (2016): 31.
[163] Ibid., 32.
[164] Underwood, 32.

business objectives in terms of the team, organizational and shareholder level."[165]

A leader with purpose has a clearer vision, and "they are able to unify people to function beyond their business goals."[166] "A leader with purpose is not afraid of crisis, but they move forward into it, driving meaningful change."[167] A leader with purpose allows people to associate and become part of the bigger picture, giving them a sense of belonging.[168] In addition, in the body of leadership, "purpose is the heart of leadership."[169] Linda had learned from Dr. Hightower's courses that her life had a purpose, and it was based on her productivity. She had learned that her performance in life was directly related to the health of her inner self.

Passion

Leadership effectiveness is intertwined with a passion to lead. "Passion flourishes when leaders experience work-life with openness, engage followers and try new ideas."[170] "They have the opportunity to explore what others would deny, the passion to entertain their doubts, and the wisdom to be unafraid of their intuition."[171] When work is driven by passion, high job performance becomes easier to sustain. In fact," A leader has to be true to what he or she is good at doing, unlocking the inner passion to make decisions and lead others."[172] In fact, passion can be contagious if it is practiced, and "it can cause

---

[165] Ibid.
[166] Ibid., 31.
[167] Cashman, 7.
[168] Ibid.
[169] Ibid.
[170] Omar Khan, "Liberating Passion," *Leadership Excellence* (2008): 12.
[171] James R. Fisher Jr., "Leadership as Great Ideas," *Leadership Excellence* (2006): 14.
[172] Alex Connock, "Your Leadership Passion," *INSEAD Articles* (2015).

leaders to make those around them passionate as well."[173] Leaders can "make passion happen by behaving their way to a vision," such as by creating a culture of passion.[174]

Besides, "leadership is about human beings and their experiences, not about heartless processes that depersonalize people in organizations."[175] People want to work under and around leaders who understand what they are experiencing, possess an intuition for detecting possible problems, and care about their charges. "Effective leadership is about serving others as opposed to self-focused leadership; once again, it is serving and not dictating."[176] "Leadership passion flows when the technical elements function as stepping stones, building a stronger authentic relationship where conversation mostly matters."[177]

This was the case with Linda. She was once making routine rounds with her team, speaking with every staff member. Linda was asked by a team member if he could leave early once his assignment was completed. He told her, "My wife is having a stomach ache, and she is pregnant." Linda told the employee that he could leave, and it would okay. She also had an inner feeling that she should ask more questions about his wife's discomfort—Linda could not understand why his wife was having a stomach ache during the pregnancy, and she was concerned it indicated a deeper problem. Linda continued to have a conversation with the employee after clearing his time off, asking him if he would call the obstetrician for his wife before he left work. Linda cared about her employee, and she felt as if something was wrong with his wife's symptoms. The

---

[173] Ibid.
[174] Khan, 12.
[175] Karlene Kerfoot, "On Leadership: From Motivation to Inspiration Leadership," *Nursing Economics* (2001): 243.
[176] Ibid.
[177] Khan, 12.

employee was extremely hesitant at first, but he agreed to call for a consultation.

However, the employee had to leave a message with an answering service, and he had to wait for a return call from the obstetrician. The employee decided to leave work before receiving a return call. Sensing that the situation would soon move outside her influence, Linda asked the employee if he was going to take his wife to the emergency room. He replied, "I'm not sure." Linda was passionate about helping the employee and his wife. Something was not making sense to her as a clinician. Linda's intuition had grown stronger, and she would not leave the subject alone. Finally, the employee agreed to take his wife to the emergency room for an assessment.

Afterward, the employee called Linda with a follow-up report. Linda was fervently waiting to hear the news. The employee told Linda that she had made the right decision in suggesting for his wife to be seen by her physician. The employee's wife had emergency care that resulted in the birth of their premature baby. Linda was glad that both baby and mom were doing well. However, Linda wondered if she as a leader had not cared enough to ask questions and had not had a genuine passion for leadership and serving others, the outcome could have been negative.

In fact, the employee told Linda that the obstetrician stated his wife and baby were in great danger if they had not come into the emergency room. The incident changed Linda as a leader, making her more passionate about her interactions with others, using work as the starting foundation and allowing the passion to flow beyond. As a result, Linda and the employee's relationship had become stronger; the premature baby eventually became a healthy child and young adult.

Persistence

Effective leaders need not only purpose and passion but persistence as part of the leadership strategy. "Effective leadership is about persistence, and the ability to remain optimistic even when the end is not clearly visible."[178] It is easy to have a great idea, but implementing and getting others to follow that idea requires persistence. In addition, there is no option to quit when it comes to leadership effectiveness: if something is not properly operating, change directions as many times as necessary until it is producing the optimal result. "Persistence is a state of mind, therefore it can be cultivated."[179] However, persistence is a result of certain factors:[180]

- ☐ Having an understanding of one's purpose, being able to know why he or she exists on the earth.[181]
- ☐ Having a desire, being able to concentrate on it creates persistence.[182]
- ☐ Being able to rely on self-ability to complete projects.[183]
- ☐ Planning and organizing.[184]
- ☐ Forming it as a habit, "the mind absorbs and becomes a part of the daily experience upon which it feeds."[185]

Whatever it takes to get the best performance, leaders must be persistent and diligent to the cause. Yet, being

---

[178] Arshavskiy, 11.
[179] Jeffrey Gitomer, "What's The Reason Some Persist until They Win and Others Quit?" *Grand Rapids Business Journal* (2016): 13.
[180] Ibid.
[181] Ibid.
[182] Ibid.
[183] Ibid.
[184] Ibid.
[185] Ibid.

proactive in turbulent times requires courage.[186] In fact, leaders must understand that facing issues that provoke fear will eliminate fear among groups in the long run.[187] "A leader's persistence is a measure of his or her belief in his or herself."[188] Just as practice makes an athlete better, persistence makes a leader more effective. As seen in the story with Linda and her employee's wife pregnancy, it was persistence that produced a good outcome for his family. Linda refused to ignore warning signs, and she began to ask more questions about his wife's condition.

Communication

In an era with frequent social media utilization, which has forever changed how people communicate with each other, communication has turned from face to face interaction and towards sending messages in shorthand form. Leadership effectiveness requires excellent communication skills to be present, especially in crisis situations. Most effective leaders have mastered the art of communication through multiple mediums. "They tend to be excellent communicators."[189] They listen reflectively to others' thoughts and are heavily engaged in private discussions.[190] They understand what people expect from their leadership style.[191]

In addition, effective leaders communicate and ensure followers are recognized for their contribution to the team.[192] They provide clear objectives, and they are usually fruitful in

---

[186] Richard Dobbins and Barrie O. Pettman, "Give Leadership," *Equal Opportunities International* (1997): 21.
[187] Dobbins and Pettman, 21.
[188] Ibid.
[189] Dobbins and Pettman, 23.
[190] Ibid.
[191] Ibid.
[192] Ibid.

getting buy-in from their team.[193] If the team or leader is in a new group, the leaders should approach the team with expectations from both sides, setting the tone at the outset of the meeting. Clarity and understanding is the key to effective communication. "Whether the leader is communicating with co-workers, followers, external or internal customers, effective communication is required at all times."[194] "Few people would dispute that regular communication in an organization is a must, good communication is two-way."[195]

For instance, Linda was working with an employee, and she noticed that every time she proceeded to speak, the employee would interrupt her thoughts. Some would call the employee's behavior *finishing one's sentence, knowing it all, not listening*, or *not being in the moment*. Linda realized the employee's interruptions were placing a strain on the conversations between her and her team. The employee was an impulsive thriller. She enjoyed the excitement of the day, she had a problem remaining still, and she wanted something to happen or else she could not function. Linda needed a task to be completed within a certain timeframe. Linda decided to ask the employee to perform the task. While Linda was reviewing the instructions with the employee, she noticed the employee's body language and verbal response. The employee was constantly interrupting her and saying, "I know it."

Linda realized that employee was not listening to her. Effective communication requires both the sender and receiver to listen while exchanging dialogue. It is hard to listen if another individual is talking at the same time a leader is talking. The employee completed the wrong task, and Linda was not surprised. Linda had a discussion with the employee and told her that the employee made the error because of a lack of listening skills. Linda said, "We failed to communicate with each other."

---

[193] Ibid.
[194] Bobbie Hayes, "Keep Smilin," *Rough Notes* (2006): 118.
[195] Sarah Cook and Steve Macaulay, "Facing Up to Blind-Spots," *Training Journal* (2015): 48.

In the future, Linda made sure effective communication was present among team members by having the employee summarize their discussion prior to leaving the conversation as part of the strategy. The employee improved her listening, she did not interrupt others as much, and she learned how to slow down from being an impulsive thriller. Linda made it known to the employee that "good communication is important for a department to run smoothly."[196] One commonality among all business industries is the need to rightly communicate. "Leadership and communication are always together, and without effective communication, there is no good leadership."[197]

Leadership Compass

Just as ships use a navigation system to chart their courses, leaders use a leadership compass to navigate through decisions, processes, and people. The leadership compass is built on a "leader's philosophy:" the "personal mission statement" for their work life.[198] Well, what shapes an individual's leadership compass? Everyone has different thoughts on being in power and leading people. Some leaders take the role as a serious one, staying concerned with people's needs and their organization's effectiveness and efficiency.

However, the leadership compass starts with a personal mission statement—the matter of the heart. What kind of person are you as a leader? Or what kind of leader are you as a person? The personal mission statement should describe the answers to these questions in one individual definition. It should give those under your leadership a chance to know

---

[196] Louise Van der Does and Stephen J. Calderia, "Effective Leaders Champion," *Nation's Restaurant News* (2006): 20.
[197] Van der Does and Calderia, 20.
[198] Ed Ruggero and Dennis F. Haley, "The Leader's Compass, 2nd ed.," *Academy Leadership* (2005): 103.

your vision and how you are going to get there. The employee should always get insight into their leader's heart and mind.

The statement must be clear and concise, leaving no room for misinterpretation.

The followings are examples of personal mission statements:

- ☐ To inspire, encourage, transform, and support others in being the best person.
- ☐ To genuinely assist others in living their lives to the fullest.

It must be developed with confidence and subject to change as needed. It is who you are when no one is looking, and when no one is supporting you as a leader. As a leader, the only person that you can truly change is yourself. In the midst of navigation, "leaders need to keep the balance of conveying purpose and direction with the attitude to change course midway if it's required."[199]

In addition, the leadership compass motivates self-awareness and self-examination as a leader. Looking inwardly daily is the beginning of leadership effectiveness. Knowing yourself and adjusting to others' behaviors will keep you on course in leadership positions. So many leaders are faithful in hanging their accomplishments on the walls in their office, the degrees and awards a constant reminder of what they endured in their quest toward leadership. Yet, so many leaders leave the degrees on the walls and miss the opportunity to hang them in their hearts, which prompts them to invest and care for others. What is the benefit of having a degree with dead works? "Leaders should widen their perspective on how to be successful through investing time in others' development, creating a win and win for everyone."[200]

---

[199] Vikram Bhalla and Xavier Sebastian, "Navigating with a Leadership Compass," *Businessline* (2012).
[200] Ibid.

A Leadership Strategy

Thus, in Linda's case, she had enrolled in a college program geared toward working adults. It was an accelerated program with a five-week course rotation. Linda was enthusiastic about going to school with adult learners like herself, working full-time in the day hours and attending classes at night. The program was centered on business administration. The class size was small, approximately eight students. During the enrollment process, Linda had several classes waived as a result of work experience. She worked exceptionally hard to complete all courses within the timeframe while trying to maintain balance at work and home. The classes were informative and helpful, and Linda often applied the material she learned at work the following day. Linda and her classmates exchanged work experiences among each other, both contributing to and gleaning from the classes' topics.

However, there appeared to be a common theme among the students involving some frustrations with the leadership office. The students had several discussions about the leadership office giving different information about grades, student's requirements, and graduation. The leadership office had struggled with a turnover in their staff, and an inexperienced person was appointed as an interim leader. The students were receptive to the new structure, but they did not understand the gap in communication given to students. They compared notes among themselves, and they decided to be proactive about the situation.

As a result of her classmates' and her own unrest, Linda made an appointment to see the leader of the program. Linda wanted to help her classmates with the graduation requirements, since only eight of them shared the same degree path and only one student so far had clearance for graduation. The leader agreed to meet with Linda. She made sure that she was prepared for the meeting, taking all the notes from her classmates since they could not make the meeting. Upon entering the leader's office, Linda was amazed at the wall, covered with so many accomplishments. *He is definitely the right person to help us*, she said to herself. This man had so many degrees, and Linda wanted just one. The leader listened to Linda's concerns, and he agreed to help all students meet the graduation requirements. Linda was relieved and happy to deliver the good news to her fellow classmates.

However, as the graduation date approached, Linda and her classmates did not hear from the leader. They became even more concerned, but Linda remained hopeful and decided to call the leader. He never returned her calls. Linda made another appointment to meet with the leader, and his secretary agreed to let him know about Linda's next meeting. Linda arrived early at the leader's office, and she had to wait until his secretary was finished with another student before getting assistance. After waiting for a long period of time, Linda was told that the leader could not meet with her since he had a conference call. *Wow*, Linda thought to herself. She told the secretary, "Okay, please let him know that I would like to speak with him if it is possible. Thank you." The secretary agreed to give the message to the leader. One week before graduation, Linda's classmates began to give up, since they were still short of the requirements to graduate.

Linda, the only student, tried to call the leader again, but he never responded to her messages; she soon realized that the leader was avoiding the students. It was unsettling to all involved. Out of eight students, only one was cleared for graduation; this did not keep up a successful graduation rate for the program. At this point, some of Linda's classmates dropped from the program, and some determined to continue trying to obtain the requirements for degree completion. Linda and her classmates supported the one student who graduated on schedule; they were pleased with her success. Linda recalled sitting in the leader's office and admiring his accomplishments on the wall. Linda knew that the leader had a chance to make a difference in her life, and he did not even try to help her or her classmates through their education. The leader's actions appeared to say, "I have my degree; you need to get your degree." Linda used the experience as a learning moment to further her leadership education, helping as many people as possible along the way. There were several takeaways that Linda, as a leader, had obtained such as the importance of integrity. If you tell your staff that you are going to do something, you need to keep your word or tell them the truth about not keeping your word. Linda had learned about taking a stand for right issues in life, even if it involves a higher authority figure. Linda had learned about the importance of having a team approach and sharing information with others. Linda sent a letter to the president of the college concerning her experience. Linda received a phone call from the vice president to address the issues and a letter with apologies from the dean of the program.

Blind Spots

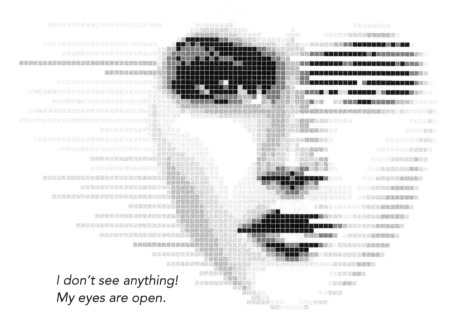

I don't see anything! My eyes are open.

Leaders can be the best in their career and still have no idea that they are missing the mark in leadership. Blind spots can be a reason for missing the mark; "this can be due to their inability to recognize when they are dealing with an ethical question or to fully understand the consequences of the ethical decisions they are making."[201] The human side of leadership struggles with "what the leader wants to do in comparison to what the leader should do."[202] "Blind spots show up in a leader's outlook and thinking, in his attitudes, behaviors, and actions when they least expect it to occur."[203] Blind spots are those issues that leaders are not aware of within themselves—flaws or irritants that other people can see. "A leader can be quite qualified, competent, skilled and knowledgeable, but if he could overcome a certain blind spot, he would be a valuable leader in the organization."[204]

However, when "an individual identifies, examine and take actions on his or her blind spots," it becomes a huge deal.[205] "Having conversations about blind spots are intended to expose any hidden areas at an individual, team and organizational level for a chance to make improvements."[206] "Some leaders are unmindful to the magnitudes of their wrong behavior on people who are impacted, they are blinded."[207] "Most people have inbuilt bias and prejudices which desire to reinforce the status quo and to stop alarm bells or contradictory information."[208] Some people do not know about their fatal flaw until

---

[201] Kevin Duggan, "Ethical Blind Spots," *Public Management* (2018): 2.
[202] Ibid.
[203] Nathaniel Stewart, "Free Yourself of Bind Spots: Five Steps Will Help You Overcome Mental Blocks to Success," *Nation's Business* (pre-1986, 1960): 86.
[204] Ibid.
[205] Sarak Cook and Steve Macaulay, "Facing Up to Bind-Spots," *Training Journal* (2015): 46.
[206] Ibid.
[207] Ibid., 48.
[208] Cook and Macaulay, 47.

it is brought to their attention. They will continue to make the same mistakes unless they see their blind spots or someone else points out their blind spots to them.

Linda, for example, was known to be professional while on duty at work. Linda went to work prepared and willingly performed any assignment provided by her manager. Linda did not joke around much since she was working in healthcare, and people's lives were impacted by her decision-making process. Linda was a sacrificial employee, always working the holidays so other leaders could spend time with their families. She did not mind helping out in these ways; she really did not want her boss to be concerned about the team and felt that things were under control when team members were scarce. Linda spent time helping others throughout holiday shifts, and even from home, Linda had called employees to check on them. Linda thought that she was performing well.

However, when Linda received her annual performance, it contained evidence of a blind spot. The overall tone of the evaluation was positive, but there was a comment from a colleague that echoed throughout Linda's mind: "Linda appeared to be angry when she was not angry." Linda's boss used the comment to magnify the blind spot and emphasized that it was an area for growth and development. Linda asked herself, *How could someone say those things about me? I am not angry, but I am a little frustrated.*

Whatever Linda's feelings were at the moment, she had to now deal with others' perceptions of her emotions. Linda had to take a self-examination of herself, looking for the blind spot that her boss magnified. She realized that she was wearing her stressed emotions on her face, and her body language probably conveyed the same message. She resolved to change others' opinions about her; she was not an angry woman. Linda decided to smile more and become less serious about small things in life. Linda made a conscious effort to smile before entering work so others could see that she was not an angry woman. Linda had to accept the blind spot, and she used it to become a better person and not a bitter person.

Summary: Building Block Four

Leading others in the right manner and producing desirable outcomes are products of leadership effectiveness. Leaders must understand purpose, passion, persistence, communication, leadership compass, and blind spots; this ultimately leads to their leadership effectiveness. Knowing the reason for an individual's existence on earth brings meaning to one's work or vocation. Knowing how to maintain on course in the face of opposition can strengthen leadership skills using persistence. Having a passion for leading makes the performance easier and profitable. Effective communication is essential for great leaders; they must be willing to utilize reflecting listening skills. Leaders must invest in their leadership through their inner compass, beliefs, and values system. A leadership compass allows them to manage people, processes, and decisions. Leadership can create blind spots; unless blind spots are addressed, they can destroy an individual's destiny. Leaders can miss the mark in leadership if blinders are present. These practices can develop and improve overall efficiency and effectiveness for leaders.

Chapter 5

Measuring Leadership Effectiveness and Efficiency

Organizations need to invest in their leaders' effectiveness—effective leaders strengthen an organization's culture. Regardless of the leadership style, every leader wants to be successful in their role. No one dreams of being a failure or misleading others; nevertheless, undesirable things happen when people are not educated about leadership. However, it takes planning and investing in oneself as a leader to become effective and efficient. It is not a hard process, but it requires consistent effort on the part of both leaders and organizations. When it comes to leadership effectiveness and efficiency, these characteristics need to be measured. How can an individual's leadership effectiveness be measured? Are there tools in place for measurement? Some many people think they are doing well as leaders, but how are they measuring their effectiveness? Are they are relying on their good name, reputation, or work ethic for measuring effectiveness? The Bible says, "Never be wise in your own sight" (Romans 12:16, English Standard Version). Leaders need to know what makes them effective and stop guesstimating when it comes to making a mark in people's lives.

There are specific tools for organizations and leaders to adopt for measuring leadership effectiveness such as competencies, leadership index, questionnaires, 360 feedback, interviews, focus groups, references, annual performance, and return demonstration approaches. Whatever leadership role an individual occupies within an organization, there is always a helpful assessment they can use; there is always room for improvement in every leader's work and home life. Leaders never reach that imaginary ultimate leadership point—growth and development is forever, an ongoing procedure. While some leaders are good at being a leader, some leaders struggle with the process of leading, and they probably do not openly admit the blindness or denial. Yet, there is help for their ineffectiveness.

Competency

Most positions require a specific skill set and knowledge base for the possible candidate. Even if the business is personally founded and operated, there is an expected level of expertise to achieve success. Quintana et al. state that workplaces specifically search for skilled employees—they must have a workforce that has the necessary experience and wisdom, as well as necessary charisma and interactive skills.[209] Organizations can thus utilize competencies assessment tools for onboarding new leaders and an ongoing screening tool for leadership effectiveness. These assessments can analyze the potential of today held by the leaders of tomorrow—in other words, "competency assessment tools provide means to identify attitudes,

---

[209] Carmen Delia Davila Quintana, Jose-Gines Mora Ruiz, and Luis E. Vila, "Competencies Which Shape Leadership," *International Journal of Manpower* (2014): 514.

and experiences of actual leaders producing evidence about the person's abilities needed to become a better leader at work."[210]

Organizations have standard competencies for leadership, ensuring human leadership capital is being shaped according to their organizational culture.[211] Employers do look for specific skills that stretch across fields: interpersonal communication, a strong knowledge base, appropriate behavior, and leadership skills among peers.[212] However, some competencies can be acquired from an individual's "work experience and formal education."[213] In fact, "the competencies possessed by a leader when they first entered into the workforce" are most likely to become the building foundation for their leadership effectiveness to develop over time.[214] Competencies are proof that an organization has properly screened and monitored leaders for their influence over other people; they are producing the optimal outcomes as a leader. Since complexities are driven by change itself, organizations need leaders who have amazing skills to overcome challenges.[215]

For instance, Linda found herself desiring another professional position. She understood the requirements for obtaining the position, prepared for the interview, and wanted to meet the criteria. Linda was given an interview with behavior questions, measuring competency in the area of leadership. The questions were grouped into categories of paying attention to details, communication, decision-making process, creativity, conflict resolution, delegation, and teamwork. Linda realized the panel interviewers were looking for a certain style

---

[210] Ibid., 518
[211] Ibid.
[212] Anonymous, "What Does It Take to Lead?" *Healthcare Leadership Alliance* (2006): 79.
[213] Delia Davila Quintana, Mora Ruiz, and Vila, 518.
[214] Ibid.
[215] Anonymous, 78.

of leadership based on competency to fit with their organizational culture. The questions were not open-ended, but rather descriptive or scenario-based with different turns; the answers had to be lengthy but complete in thought.

Linda wanted to leave an impression on the panel of leaders even if she did not get the position. In fact, she wanted to show that a performance of leadership was being portrayed by her and by the panel within the interview. Linda wanted to challenge the panel to think about leadership, not just the position. She measured each panel member's competency silently. Linda was measuring them as leaders as they were assessing her for the position. Did Linda want to work under their leadership? The panel was the frontline for the organization, representing the culture as a whole. *Is this what a leader can expect?* Linda wondered. *What kind of leaders are within this organization?* Linda had questions as the interview concluded—she was amazed to hear the panel views on leadership expectations. Linda had to think about being part of that specific leadership team. Linda knew she had the required skill set; she was competent and confident that she could perform the role.

Leadership Index

Another method to measure effectiveness is by using a leadership index. It is a tool created to measure different components that lead to success or effectiveness in leadership.[216] The tool consists of questions about oneself as a leader and how one responds in different situations within the organization.[217] Yiannis Koutsoumaris of Inwards Coaching states, "The results can be presented as a scorecard format with areas covering

---

[216] "The Leadership Index," *Inwards Advanced Coaching* (2018), https://inwards.gr/aksiologikes-ektimisis.
[217] Ibid.

leadership performance, productivity, employee engagement, commitment, measuring the emotional and cognitive state of the leader."[218] The tool is created to "assess a leader's self-awareness and blind spots" for improvement in the long run.[219]

According to Castellano, leadership value as a whole needs to be thought of as interrelating skills.[220] Leadership needs standardized competency standards for organizations to use in measuring a leader's effectiveness.[221] The leadership index can concentrate on either the leader or the organization, providing data on good leaders' qualities.[222] The leadership index can provide a pathway for a better return on investment in leadership for the organization.[223] Besides, ineffective leadership can derail the mission and culture of an organization; it must be identified and corrected.

Such was the case with Linda: she used an instrument provided by the organization to measure her effectiveness over her team. It was a common practice for her and her employees. Linda was motivated to share her thoughts and use her voice to prompt positive change within the company. In fact, it was the best time for employees to speak up about issues that need a little more attention using a survey. However, as a leader, survey review was a time when the criticism was likely to be evident, and thick skin was required to endure harsh comments. The organizational instrument gave insight into the achievements and problems within a group of people. It was often broken down into the leader, direct report, and their

---

[218] Ibid.
[219] Ibid.
[220] Stephanie Castellano, "A New Yardstick for Leadership the Value of Leadership Capital Index: Realizing the Market Value of Leadership," *Talent Development* (2015): 74.
[221] Ibid.
[222] Ibid.
[223] Ibid.

relationship to the organization as a whole. However, the results were seriously used for action planning and improvements.

Linda noticed that on a certain questionnaire, the results provided a section labeled *Leadership Index*. What was this new terminology about? Linda gathered that this index represented her own ability to properly lead within her current role. The questions were answered by those under Linda's authority. There were questions such as the following:

- ☐ Does the leadership behave in ways that are indicative of the core values of the organization?
- ☐ Does leadership take a genuine interest in the needs of the staff?
- ☐ Does leadership communicate good or bad news in a timely manner?
- ☐ Does leadership allow input from staff in the decision-making process?
- ☐ Does leadership create a culture where staff can speak up without being fearful of backlash?
- ☐ Does leadership follow through with their deeds, words or thoughts?

Linda's score was ranked against other leaders within the organization—the average leadership index. Linda wanted to make sure she was fitting into the organization's culture, and the score reflected her effectiveness. Linda's score was above the average leadership effectiveness score for the overall organization.

Yet, Linda had areas to maintain and areas to make some adjustments, but in the end, what really mattered was Linda's willingness to become a better leader. If the leader does not have a desire to make changes within him or herself, it will not work for the group. In fact, the change will only be superficial and short-lived within the culture. Leadership effectiveness is ongoing, and it starts with being honest with oneself about one's flaws. If you are not giving a great performance today, you can perform better tomorrow. There is always a chance to do better.

360 Feedback

The performance process starts with a manager requesting input from the leader through a self-assessment. The leader is given a chance to properly assess him or herself by providing the feedback. The manager sends a request to obtain 360 feedback information from the leader's peers, direct reports and other team members. Pfay et al. remind leaders, "The more complete the insight into a leader's performance, the more likely he or she will understand what areas need to be improved."[224] The results of the assessment are tantamount to the leader learning how to change their communications strategies and grow.[225]

Once the information is returned, the manager reviews the comments for any unprofessional verbiage. The manager has the choice to insert, correct and delete final comments as necessary. The comments are meant to build a great leader, making them more effective, so they must be accurate and fair. "People need to be trained in the art of giving and receiving feedback to prevent uncertainty and conflict among team members," Pfay et al. remind us.[226] The manager should meet with the leader to share the comments, giving him or her a chance speak about the findings and a chance to create a strategy for effectiveness. In fact, "Some studies show that 360-feedback can improve the performance of a leader."[227]

---

[224] Pfay, Kay, Nowack, and Ghorpade, 54.
[225] Brandon Kilburn and Tommy Cates, "Leader Behavior: Gatekeeper to Voluntary Upward Feedback," *Management Research Review* (2010): 901.
[226] Pfay, Kay, Nowack, and Ghorpade, 54.
[227] Lawrence, 5.

Measuring leadership effectiveness can be accomplished through both negative and positive feedback, comments aimed to bring out the best in a leader. Everyone takes pride in receiving feedback that is uplifting for their personal and work life, but they might struggle with receiving feeback that reveals a blind spot or possible flaw. However, all feedback is useful—both positive and negative. Feedback can make an individual become bitter or better depending on the leader's growth and maturity. "Most organizations utilize 360-feedback as an effective performance management tool" and a general method to collect indirect feedback about peers, superiors, and direct reports.[228] An organization's leadership must ensure the 360 feedback is used for the purpose it was designed, not as a punitive process.[229]

Lawrence notes that 360 tool specifications should match with the behavior specifications for leaders already in a given organization.[230] The 360 feedback is often sent from an appraisal standpoint to the employee's peers, seeking input from different people.[231] "The premise behind 360-feedback," say Pfay et al., "is that the people working closely with an employee see that person's behavior in settings and circumstance that a supervisor may not."[232]

These standards and measurements work together to provide the studied individual with a valuable grasp of their own effect on peers.[233]

For instance, on Linda's appraisal, she received comments

---

[228] Bruce Pfay, Ira Kay, Kenneth M. Nowack, and Jai Ghorpade, "Does 360-Degree Feedback Negatively Affect Company Performance?" *HR Magazine* (2002): 54.

[229] Ibid.

[230] Paul Lawrence, "Building Great 360 Feedback Program," *Training and Development* (2015): 5.

[231] Pfay, Kay, Nowack, and Ghorpade, 54.

[232] Ibid.

[233] Paul Lawrence, "Building Great 360 Feedback Program," *Training and Development* (2015): 5.

from the 360 feedback in the strength assessment section about her ability to help others perform at their highest skill level, seeing the potential in them to be the best employee. In the growth and development section, Linda needed to become more firm in disagreeing with her peers in healthy conflict. Linda used the comments as a goal for the next appraisal period. She wanted to ensure that she mastered the area of healthy conflict, developing more in the things critiqued. However, Linda had to agree with the comments for development to transpire.

Questionnaire

Another useful tool to measure leadership effectiveness is a questionnaire. It is necessary for employees to think highly of their leaders in order for those leaders to truly succeed.[234] Toward figuring out their opinions of their leaders, employees must be aware that "the evaluation of their leader's effectiveness can be described as their overall satisfaction with the leader and the perception of strong leadership."[235] However, "for some organizations, assessing the effectiveness of a leader is often a difficult exercise."[236] Assessments succeed or fail sometimes based largely on whether they are "influenced by organizational politics, and not standard based,"[237] causing a discrepancy for authentic leadership effectiveness. The questionnaire provides an alternative method for unreliable screening methods for leadership effectiveness.[238] Oyinlade

---

[234] Gesche Drescher, "Delegation Outcomes: Perceptions of Leaders and Follower's Satisfaction," *Journal Of Managerial Psychology* (2017): 3.
[235] Ibid.
[236] Olu A. Oyinlade, "A Method of Assessing Leadership Effectiveness: Introducing the Essential Behavioral Leadership Qualities Approach," *Performance Improvement Quarterly* (2006): 25.
[237] Ibid.
[238] Ibid.

insists, "It can be designed so leaders are precisely evaluated on specific behavioral characteristics and their leadership ratings are standard based."[239]

The questionnaire provides pertinent information if it properly constructed.[240] It is informative and beneficial.[241] In creating a questionnaire, "the organization must consider if a standardized assessment can be used or if they need to design one to fits its leadership needs."[242] The information needs to be clearly defined for the purpose and the intent in which it will be used,[243] leadership effectiveness. "The organization must decide to use both open-ended and close-ended questions,"[244] allowing more options for data collection. The questionnaire should be administered to the leader's direct reports in a set timeframe. The organization should determine a certain response rate for accuracy. The results should be shared with the leader evaluated.

Focus Groups

Group discussion, agreement, and disagreement sometimes afford leaders and their followers more clarity than individual assessments.[245] "One advantage of a focus group," notes Pam Jackson, "is having a chance to obtain a large number of employees participate in a subject in a short period."[246] It allows employees to support each other and their leader during the

---

[239] Ibid.
[240] John Maher Jr. and Edward C. Kur, "Constructing Good Questionnaires," *Training and Development Journal* (1983): 100.
[241] Ibid.
[242] Ibid.
[243] Maher Jr. and Kur, 100.
[244] Ibid.
[245] Pam Jackson, "Focus Group Interviews as a Methodology," *Nurse Researcher* (1998): 72.
[246] Ibid.

group discussion, adding more value to the topic about their leader. It gives them the opportunity to learn something different about their leader. Successful focus group often have a non-threatening atmosphere in which to occur, remain small in number, bring together compatible employees, and fall under the authority of some sort of chaperone.[247]

In addition, "focus groups are used in combination with other methods."[248] Linda's team had undergone a survey where its leaders' effectiveness was being questioned. Linda's team was expressing some dissatisfaction among its leaders. As a result, Linda's team was scheduled to meet in focus groups to provide an in-depth overview of their concerns about their leaders' ineffectiveness. The focus groups consisted of at least five to six employees, and no leaders were allowed in the discussions. The facilitator scheduled the focus groups' discussion for one hour. The environment was relaxed, supporting employees' honest concerns. The survey data and information provided by the employees was shared with leaders to enhance the effectiveness of their leaders.

Interview

Leaders can never have enough or too much information to improve their effectiveness. In fact, using different tools together might be the optimal selection for them. The interviews take place between the leader being assessed and their superior or designee. Interviews are an informative tool to use; the interviewer and interviewee can benefit from the interaction, getting real-time formation and meaningful discussion. Interviews can be done with single or multiple people, depending on the level of content being discussed. Leadership effectiveness

---

[247] Ibid.
[248] David L. Morgan, "Focus Groups," *Annual Review of Sociology* (1996): 133.

might be a reason for the leader to make behavioral changes, which need to be discussed privately with the leader, not on a panel. Brown et al. go so far as to say, "The way negative feedback is communicated is important, as it impacts an employee's interpretation and response to the feedback."[249]

Importantly, Brown et al. also note that potential employee assessors must be aware of the project before they are asked in to speak about their leader—no surprises for the contributors in leadership assessments.[250] The meeting should be conducted in a less intimating atmosphere, giving the leader liberty to provide and respond to the feedback. It should not be longer than an hour, since the goal is to obtain information, not to become a griping session. "Information interviews are conducted to give the information needed to effectively perform," Boissoneau reminds readers.[251] "Much of what the leader needs to learn about the organization and their needs can come from the interview."[252] There should be a connecting point for both the interviewer and the leader in the meeting, a shared vision or goal.[253]

References

Gathering information from people who know the leader on a personal or professional level can be valuable. "Professional references are people who worked with the leader and know them from a professional position," says MacFadden.[254] On the

---

[249] Michelle Brown, Carol T. Kulik, and Victoria Lim, "Managerial Tactics for Communicating Negative Performance Feedback," *Personnel Review* (2016): 970.
[250] Ibid., 973.
[251] Robert Boissoneau, "Planning and Conducting An Information Interview," *Hospital Materiel Management Quarterly* (1986): 17.
[252] Ibid.
[253] Ibid.
[254] David MacFadden, "A Guide to Resume References," *Alberni Valley Times* (2003): 17.

other hand, personal references know the leaders deeply, but have encountered them mostly outside of work contexts.[255] However, "to maximize the odds of collecting targeted feedback, the specific area should be defined for usage."[256] References allow organizations to collect data with a leader's knowledge for their effectiveness. Since leaders are often leading projects, references can provide insight about their strengthens and weaknesses.

In fact, "it can be lonely at the top, and if a leader does not seek frequent feedback from their workforce on how to manage people, processes, and other key aspects of the business, he or she can become more isolated."[257] Leadership is about being part of a team, efficiently working with other people to bring about desired goals. References are important to fleshing out the pictures of who the leader is;[258] the references just need to know the areas of concentration, such as the leader's strong and weak points, achievements, and personal values. References are important, since curious organizations wishing to improve must truly know the character of their employed leaders.[259] It can help them make a big investment in their organizational culture.

Performance Appraisal

Performance appraisal is a reflection of an individual's life at work. Spending countless hours within an organization, people need to know if they are aligned with the organization's strategic plan or moving in a different direction. Performance appraisal allows leaders to be screened on an annual basis for

---

[255] Ibid.
[256] Morey Stettner, "Lead Better by Asking for Feedback," *Investor's Business Daily* (2014): A07.
[257] Ibid.
[258] Ibid.
[259] Ibid.

progress. Yet, "some organizations perform appraisal quarterly or semi-annually."[260] Say Plesis and Neikerk,

> Performance appraisal has been seen as a vital process aimed at improving employee performance, which yields organization efficiency. Performance appraisal is also used as a method to determine salary increases and job promotion. An organization must create a framework for which performance appraisal is conducted. (8–9)

"The framework should consist of building a performance improvement plan and implementing it with leadership coaching."[261] Performance appraisal can be used as a training mechanism, "looking back and moving ahead to fulfill future objectives."[262] The content on the performance appraisal should not be a surprise to the leader at the time of discussion—everyone deserves a grace period to make the required changes for effectiveness.

For instance, Linda had learned that from an employee's perspective, there is usually a negative association with a performance appraisal. Linda dreaded meeting with her direct boss for the performance appraisal, knowing it was that time of the year to just go through the motions of review. Linda often felt as if her boss really did not care about her growth and development. At the beginning of the appraisal process, the direct boss sent a self-assessment to Linda for her input. Linda had to examine and rate herself according to the core values of the organization and the competencies of her current position. Linda never had a problem with the self-assessment, knowing it was to bring about internal change and make her a

---

[260] Donald L. Kirkpatrick, "Integrating Training and Performance Appraisal," *Training* (2012): 12.
[261] Kirkpatrick, 12.
[262] Ibid.

better person, employee, colleague, and leader. The appraisal process continued with the direct boss sending 360 feedback tools to others who worked with Linda and under her authority. Then, the direct boss had to complete his evaluation of Linda's competency and leadership skill set. The boss had to set goals and objectives for Linda's upcoming year, along with Linda's input. After completing all of the parts to the appraisal, the direct boss had to schedule a meeting with Linda to review the appraisal.

After the many appraisals, Linda met with her direct boss. It would only last for ten minutes. The direct boss would start the discussion: "Please read the comments and let me know if you have any questions." Linda did not understand why her work life seemed so unimportant to her boss, so she asked her direct boss, and he denied the assumption. Linda wanted to complete the best performance possible, so his job was much easier, he said. Linda wanted her direct boss to appreciate her effort throughout the year and tell her about it. Linda just wanted to hear her direct boss say, "Thank you for all you do for me and our staff." Linda had known the power of thank you. It would make an individual perform better, go the extra mile, stay longer at work, and become excited about doing any tasks. In fact, "Most of us liked to be thanked, especially when the sentiment is sincere."[263] "For that reason, 'thank you' is one of the most powerful phrases in the world."[264] Linda reviewed the appraisal, read the comments, but she never heard the phrase, " Thank you." Linda asked her boss, "What about the college courses that I had taken? Do I get credit for taking them?" The boss replied, "Oh yeah, I would have to redo the entire appraisal to add them, so I can add them the next time."

Linda was stunned at this sloppy excuse. Linda was totally

---

[263] Kate Zabriskie, "Using the Power of 'Thank You' To Get What You Want: Influencing Others Made Easier," *Personal Excellence Essentials* (2018).
[264] Ibid.

disappointed with the meeting, even though the appraisal process was professionally structured. "I was expecting to hear 'thank you.'" So, Linda added her comments to the appraisal, and she thanked her direct boss for his brief time before excusing herself. Just the power of a simple 'thank you' can influence individuals and soften them towards the thankful speaker.[265] At least Linda tried to move her direct boss in a different direction. Linda made plans to approach the process differently in the next appraisal period. She would request a longer period of time to have a more beneficial discussion for her leadership effectiveness.

Suggestions in Getting the Most from the Appraisal Process:

- ☐ Have an open mindset, eliminate fear
- ☐ Prepare ahead of time
- ☐ Review past appraisal, looking at previous goals, complete any requested information
- ☐ Bring a list of questions-goals
- ☐ Be present in the moment, no distractions, listen
- ☐ Meet in a positive atmosphere at the right time
- ☐ Make it a great experience

Return Demonstration

Return demonstration is allowing someone to show a specific skill after having some formal education, training, or experience. Along with the previous measuring tools for leadership effectiveness, there is nothing better than return demonstration skills from the leader. "The ability of an individual to

---

[265] Zabriskie.

perform job responsibilities is part of the competency checklist,"[266] and organizations can allow the individual to perform the competency checklist through return demonstration in a simulation or assessment center. "Leaders can be formally evaluated by trained observers on their demonstration of leadership competencies in a series of activities," says Scott Allen, and "Leaders can receive onsite feedback on their strengths and weakness to identify training needs, managerial talent, and performance in relation to other participating leaders."[267]

Gorwing et al. conclude that assessment tools are a valuable way for getting to know a leader and their future possibilities.[268] Therefore, organizations should invest in them, creating an in-house center or using an external site. Locations meant for administering assessments can become cherished places, where leaders grow more fully and come face-to-face with those they lead.[269] In fact, these locations can create the space for "rich behavioral information" to emerge and begin to shape leaders.[270]

Linda's Return Demonstration

While Linda had not participated in an assessment center for leadership within an organization, she did participate in a global simulation program for a leadership course. The class was grouped into four teams with four participants each to compete with other colleges. The program was designed to push each team to start a camera business from the beginning phase while

---

[266] Edwina A. McConnell, "Competence vs. Competency," *Nursing Management* (2001): 14.
[267] Ibid.
[268] Marilyn K. Gowing, David M. Morris, Alder Seymour, and Mitchell Gold, "The Next Generation of Leadership Assessment: Some Case Studies," *Public Personnel Management* (2008): 437.
[269] Ibid.
[270] Ibid., 438.

keeping a competitive advantage over the other groups. The program was a business-strategy game, used both online and offline. Each participant was assigned roles and responsibilities for the simulation. The overall goal was to "run the company in any way they wanted"[271] to as leaders, but while ensuring particular principles were being met, operating in an efficient manner. Each team had an obligation to its shareholders and investors, establishing annual objectives for five key performance indicators (KPIs). The simulation provided weekly scorecards among the different teams. Each team had to invest their products into the four different markets. The team had to make decisions from product and design, marketing, socially responsibility, shipping, and receiving, compensation and benefits, and overseeing financial performances, the bottom line.

Summary: Building Block Five

Leaders can measure and support their effectiveness through specific tools such as competency tests, a leadership index, 360 feedback, questionnaires, focus groups, interview, references, performance appraisal, and return demonstration. Leaders think that they are doing well in their leadership performance, but it must be measured for an accurate assessment—guessing and not knowing the truth is not enough. Organizations must participate in their leaders' productivity and leadership skills. Leaders' growth and development is a continuous process, and these tools can make them better. Measuring effectiveness can eliminate barriers and blindness in the growth and development of leaders.

---

[271] Morgan W. McCall Jr., and Michael M. Lombardo, "Using Simulation for Leadership and Management Research: Through the Looking Glass," *Management Science* (pre-1986): 533.

Chapter 6

Challenges in Leadership

Great leaders do not reach their goals and success without some type of challenge. Leadership itself can be complicated, never remaining the same in different situations. Yet, great leaders did not give up, throw in the towels, or quit. They kept moving forward to improve themselves, and everything else externally followed until they reached a destination. Leadership is a journey with obstacles and stumbling blocks along the pathway. An individual who knows how to take a detour around challenges and remain on course to the final destination is a great leader. But what are some basic challenges that leaders must overcome?

Work-Life Balance

Technology has forced many people to live a "faster-paced" life, both personally and professionally.[272] Where is the bal-

---

[272] Omar Fayaz Khan and Asif Iqbal Fazili, "Work Life Balance: A Conceptual Review," *Journal of Strategic Human Resource Management* (2016): 20.

ance? Leaders are expected to be the first person in the office and the last person to leave the office, never taking a day off without checking emails or text messages. If this describes a leader you know, it is most likely they are headed towards burnout. There are only twenty-four hours in a day, but some people work more than half of the day, leaving them with little time for family and self. There must be a balance between work and home life, harmony in the midst of life and leading. "Organizations must realize the long-term benefits of well-constructed work-life balance policies for employees," Khan and Fazili state.[273] "Work-life balance is about efficiently managing the pressures between paid employment and all additional activities that are important to people such as family, community activities, voluntary work, individual growth, and spare time and amusement," add Dizaho et al.[274] Also, "it is related to an individual's psychological well-being and overall sense of harmony in life."[275] Organizations must increase awareness of the imbalance between work and personal lives, and they must provide healthy avenues to supporting their employees in a busy environment.

For instance, Linda had to develop a plan to balance technology usage for work and her personal life. She noticed that emails were frequently coming, so she decided to link it with her personal phone to maintain control of them. It sounded like a brilliant idea until Linda went home. She had more notifications come across her phone at unexpected moments such as doctor's appointment church services, shopping, family functions, etc. The sound of the notifications prompted Linda

---

[273] Ibid., 24.
[274] Ester Kadarko Dizaho, Rohani Salleh, and Azrai Abdullah, "Achieving Work Life Balance through Flexible Work Schedules and Arrangements," *Global Business and Management Research Suppl. Special Issue* (2017): 457.
[275] Kinga Hoffman-Burdzinska and Monika Rutkowska, "Work Life Balance as a Factor," *Journal of Positive Management* (2015): 93.

to respond. She was continuously monitoring her emails and not enjoying her time away from the office. She was working all the time, and it began to affect her attitude about work. Linda realized her work-life balance needed an adjustment, and she took action. She made the decision to disconnect the email linkage from *her* personal phone. She made a conscious decision to *work* in the office and *live* at home. She got her life back in order!

Fears and Failures

If you polled most individuals about their childhood dreams of becoming a leader, they would probably never mention the possibility of facing or dealing with fears or failures in the process of becoming a leader. In fact, when asked in high school about it, no one says, "My name is [___], and I want to experience failures in life." However, the truth is that life will happen, and growing leaders must learn how to survive through the pressures and live out the experiences. Most great leaders have had many great fears or great failures in their lives. It is impossible to rise to the top of your profession without experiencing some form of fear or failure; it is the norm. "Fear affects all leaders from the lead driver to Chief Executive Officer (CEO),"[276] but fear can be conquered.

Therefore, while most people struggle with the idea of being a failure, great leaders learned how to embrace the thought of never giving up. They keep trying something else until it works for them. When true leaders experience failure, they stop, reevaluate, and try a different approach—instead of quitting altogether.[277] Quitting is not an option for great

---

[276] Dana White, "How to Truly Lead: And Not Simply Manage," *Leadership Excellence Essentials* (2016): 21.
[277] Jeffrey Pfeffer and Robert L. Sutton, *The Knowing-Doing Gap: How Smart Companies Turn Knowledge into Action* (Harvard Business School

leaders; endurance to the end is the only alternative. "Great leaders overcome the fear of change, fear of failure, and the fear of being obsolete," says White.[278] White goes on to insist that while great leaders toil in the present, they never stop dreaming of the future they will create; they build up the people around them as heirs in their legacy instead of obstacles.[279] Great leaders understand that their fears and failures are the fuel needed to keep the fire burning on their leadership journey, keeping them authentic, focused, and faithful to those under their authority.

"Surely leaders do not fear, right?"[280] Linda knew many personal fears and experienced many failures. Many leaders do not think of fear when they think about leadership training.[281] Yet, "the trainer can step in very effectively to deal with it."[282] Linda always struggled with things going wrong on her leadership journey. From simple moments to difficult moments, there seemed to always be some form of opposition in both her personal and professional life. Linda recalled one of her professors saying, "All leaders are struggling with something." It was a profound statement that changed Linda's perspective on accepting opposition. Linda was one of those leaders who wanted everything to go well in everyone's life, but Linda had to learn that she could only control her choices and behaviors in life and not feel guilty when things failed, especially at work. Linda wanted her team to enjoy being at work, getting along with each other and helping others when their assignments were completed.

However, there were times when certain team members

Publishing, 2000), xii.
[278] White, 21.
[279] Ibid.
[280] Tony Hare, "Fear in Leadership: The Adrenaline Journey," *Training Journal* (2003): 30.
[281] Ibid.
[282] Ibid.

refused to be team players, causing an interruption in teamwork for an entire shift. Linda felt as if a follower's behavior was a reflection of his or her leader. Linda refused to accept this behavior as her own. In fact, uncooperative behavior was opposite of the organization's core values and Linda's personal values. Linda had to address the lack of teamwork with certain team members—her team was holding her responsible for the lack of teamwork among them. Linda had an obligation to foster a positive working environment for all employees, so she did not want to fail at providing that culture. Hare distills the idea by writing that "converting fear or opposition from a problem into a force for positive change can be a very rewarding process for both leaders and their employees."[283] Regardless of the circumstance, leaders can be overcomers of fears and failures.

Competition

Another challenge for leaders to deal with is competition. Society and reality programming have portrayed a desirable lifestyle where people in business can be "cutthroat" professionals.[284] Galt argues that corporate life is often characterized by rampant competition instead of professionalism.[285] Analysts have said for years that to be known, you must be the best in the profession, outperforming everyone else on the team. "Business competition," warns Tisch, "is similar to a struggle for survival on an island of tropical cannibals."[286] Some people will do anything to be well-known, creating their own successful moments, caring only about the person in the mirror.

---

[283] Hare, 30.
[284] Jonathan M. Tisch, "From 'Me' To 'We' Leadership," *Wall Street Journal* (2004): B2.
[285] Virginia Galt, "Cutthroat Culture in Decline," *The Globe and Mail* (2007).
[286] Tisch, B2.

However, everyone wants to be successful in life, and everyone deserves it. "Does success mean clawing your way to the top of the mountain at the expense of your competitors- so long as you do not get caught?" Tisch asks.[287] An organization is usually considered as one team with several small units collaboratively working as a whole; organizations thus should take a team approach—not an individual approach—to success. The cooperation of every level of an organization—from board members to blue-collar employees—is necessary to produce true success.[288] "Future leaders will be judged by their ability to lead by example, build loyalty, and ensure sustainability" toward this ultimate end of cooperation, says Barker.[289] "In the business environment, it is really about using good behavior along with efficient processes to drive the bottom line; there is no room for a cutthroat mentality."[290]

However, "Good leaders must spend more time looking at their own behavior and performance before they can effectively manage that of their employees."[291] There was so much work to be done, so many employees' needs to be met, Linda did not have time to compete with the new person on the block. Linda had a team approach. If the team succeeded, they all succeeded as a whole. Linda learned how to pick and choose the situation in which to compete. One new employee had a different approach: she wanted things to be done to her liking, since after all, she had a higher opinion about herself than about others.

Linda originally had respect for this new employee, but it began to change after Linda started to witness a variation in her behavior. Linda witnessed the new person's leadership

---

[287] Ibid.
[288] Ibid.
[289] Barker, "Launch of New Leadership Style for Businesses," *Illawarra Mercury* (2003): 42.
[290] Ibid.
[291] Ibid.

quest turned into a 'self-quest' in which she tried to make a big name for herself, forgetting about the people on the team. The new person began to teach others how to undermine Linda's authority and listen to only her authority. Linda found herself in competition for leading her team, but Linda was confident that she could stay on course. Linda wanted the best for the new person and her team. Linda realized that leaders could not force a relationship with their employees but instead had to honestly work toward attaining communication.[292] Linda did not want competition, but she wanted collaboration to exist among her teammates Linda decided to ask the new person for guidance on a team project in which she had known was an area of strength for the new person, Linda wanted to make things work for the overall success of her team, but it would take a bigger leader's approach. It wasn't that Linda needed the guidance, but she needed unity in leadership. After all, they were working on the same team for the same shared objectives. Linda's approach was effective and it brought the unity.

■   ■   ■

Another competing situation Linda found herself in was during the annual leadership program. Linda went once a year to meet with her colleagues on campus. The first year was extremely challenging as a student leader. Linda and her classmates were given the task of creating a group presentation as a part of the program requirement. Linda's group had a testing moment trying to form as a group. All of them were students in a leadership role within their organization. They had great ideas, but they needed just one person to orchestrate the presentation, not the entire group.

However, Linda told the group that they needed a leader

---

[292] Tisch, B2.

to provide oversight and direction for the project. Linda's comments were met with resistance. "We all are leaders, according to one classmate." Yes, that is true, but even a group leaders need a leader. Everyone wanted to be in charge, but no one wanted to follow another person. The student leaders were competing for a position to lead, so they decided to take a section of the topic to present for themselves, trying to deal with conflict without a leader, and not wanting to humble themselves. When it was time to present the project, one student did not participate as she was upset about the lack of synergy among the student leaders. There is a time and place for competition in leadership.

Missed Opportunities

Leaders like to know what is going on within their organizations. However, leaders cannot be everything to everyone, and they cannot be in all places at the same time. If there is a meeting that a leader forgot to mention or a hot topic they forgot to respond to, it is okay. Leaders must pick and choose their opportunities to lead, making a difference. Yet, "in order to seize opportunities, leaders must recognize them."[293] Sometimes there are missed opportunities in leadership such as "hearing people's stories, encouraging team members to reflect on satisfaction in their work, inviting the elephant in the room to dance, and developing yourself."[294] Robertson insists that leaders are always on and available to be approached by employees and potential assessors.[295] However, "leaders who fail to attempt to connect with people miss an opportunity to

---

[293] Dan Rockwell, "Leadership Freak: The Top 12 Missed Opportunities of Leadership," *Newstex Global Business Blogs* (2016).
[294] Ibid.
[295] Larry Roberston, "The Cost of Missed Opportunities," *Strategic Communication* (2005): 5.

build a winning team, and respectful relationships."[296] Even if leaders are faced with a missed occasion, there is a great possibility that more opportunities will come. Leaders need to be ready to embrace them.

For instance—leadership was personal for Linda. She tried to encourage everyone who needed support in their work or personal life. Linda often found herself in a hurry, moving from one point to the next, thinking about what needed to be done while performing another task. Linda was always one step ahead of the next, being not in the present but in the future. Linda was performing everything at a fast pace such as walking, eating, working, talking, and leading; then, life happened and slowed Linda down.

One day Linda was leaving a retail store, and she noticed a truck driving into the parking lot with a palm tree branch under the tire. The sight caught Linda's attention, as she thought the branch could ruin the tire. Linda wanted to let the driver know about the palm branch under the tire. Linda slowly proceeded to the truck, trying not to scare the driver. Linda began to signal the driver by waving her hand, and saying, "Hello." The driver rolled down the window, and Linda explained the condition to her. The driver said, " I know you."

Linda said, "You do?"

The driver explained their past interactions, and Linda remembered the pleasant experiences with the driver. Linda recalled giving the driver a baby gift for her unborn child in the past. Linda asked about the baby. The driver began to share her story about the son, who was now about ten years of age and had a near-drowning experience as a toddler. The child required special care since the incident. The driver had to make changes in her profession in order to take care of her son and had to work from home. The driver's story was heart-wrenching, and Linda felt the need to reach out to her

---

[296] Ibid.

on a later date. So they both exchanged information with the intent to meet for lunch or just to chat. Linda continued with her busy life and thought sometimes about when to call the driver, but it never happened. Sometime later, Linda was told about the driver's death. Linda was devastated about the news. If only Linda had called her. It was a missed opportunity to make a life-changing difference. As a result of it, Linda was no longer living a fast-paced work or personal lifestyle. Linda made a vow: no more missed opportunities. She decided to assess all of the opportunities she encountered and grasp the moment.Linda stopped wasting time and putting things off for tomorrow.

Knowing and Doing the Right Thing

Why is it difficult to do the right thing within some organizations? Organizations have created policies and procedures for employees to follow as well as standards to ensure quality products and services are provided to their customers. Organizations utilize resources to make sure their products and services meet external governing boards' standards. Most people have some formal education required for their profession. However, there still appears to be some distance between knowing the right thing to do and actually performing the right thing, which is a challenge in leadership. Unfortunately, some organization consistently see that even highly knowledgable and skilled leaders do not make morally sound choices.[297] Even worse, they stay in large corporate cultures that do not support their personal ethics—Pfeffer and Sutton ask, "Why [do] so many managers know so much about organizational performance, they discuss so many effective things about how to achieve performance, work so hard, but they are trapped in organizations that do

---

[297] Carol Kennedy, *The Knowing-Doing Gap* (Director, 2000), 167.

A Leadership Strategy

so many things they know will undermine performance?"[298] Even with the most successful organizations, there can be a problem with changing a knowledge base into productive action, a struggle in leadership.[299] "What prevented organizations led by smart people from doing things that they know they ought to do?" scholars have asked time and again.[300] Corporate cultures and not truly taking advantage or the knowledge and wisdom bases offered them by becoming as productive as they can be.[301] One reason for not practicing what they preached is a result of "fear and distrust."[302]

However, organizations must identify the seriousness of the distance, or the "knowing and doing gap,"[303] and be willing to do something about their current organizational state. It starts with leadership—top administration truly leading by example and developing a strategy to address the deficiencies. Also, leaders affect deficiencies by "creating a plan that will help better align training programs to necessary outcomes."[304] Kennedy reminds leaders that organizations in which sloppy work is passed by and blaming, it becomes the norm do nothing to help their employees keep bettering themselves.[305] Yet, there is a competitive advantage of knowing how what to do and getting the job accomplished, having the brain of the industry and using it.[306] "There is a competitive advantage of knowing how to foster cooperation, not competition, and how to drive out the fear out of

---

[298] Pfeffer and Sutton, ix.
[299] Ibid.
[300] Ibid, x.
[301] Ibid.
[302] Ibid, 109.
[303] Ibid, x.
[304] John Cox, "Closing Talent Development's Knowing-Doing Gap," *Talent Development* (2015): 78.
[305] Carol Kennedy, *The Knowing-Doing Gap* (Director, 2000), 167.
[306] Ibid.

the organization," insist Pfeffer and Sutton.[307] Organizations can close the knowing and doing gap when they place their "knowledge into action."[308]

For example, Linda's team had undergone a series of organizational surveys. The purpose was to make improvements in the future state of her team. Linda's direct boss often made jokes about not doing anything about the results. Linda recalled a meeting with her direct boss and others when the instrument results were not favorable. Linda's boss appeared to be concerned about the results in front of the other guests, but he later changed the tone after leaving the meeting. He said, "We are not going to do anything different, but copy and paste the past information on the action plan."

Linda asked, "Are you sure? We were told to come up with a plan to make things better."

Linda's boss replied, "Yep."

Linda began to struggle with her boss's decision, so she created an effective action plan for her team in spite of the boss's judgment. Linda's boss was known for saying the right thing to people, and doing another thing once they left his presence. Linda created an action plan that included both leaders and frontline staff engagement. She wanted the information to reach those under her leadership, trying to close a widening gap. While a leader cannot control whether or not another person does the right thing, they can consciously make a choice themselves to do the right thing, again and again.

---

[307] Anonymous 3, Jeffrey Pfeffer and Robert Sutton, "The Knowing-Doing Gap: How Smart Companies Turn Knowledge Into Action," *Food Management* (2000): 13.
[308] Ibid.

Unethical Behavior Continues

If people know to do right, then just do it, right? It is not that easy for some leaders. In fact, there is a huge struggle with leaders and unethical behavior in our society. It can be seen in all of the business industries. When it comes to ethics, leaders have a different opinion on what constitutes ethical behavior. "Ethics concentrates on processes and topics that direct the decision-making process in terms of what is right," say Askew et al.[309] Something that appears to be ethical for one leader might not be seen as ethical to another leader. However, even the best organizations are susceptible to both ethical and unethical behaviors routinely throughout their organizations.[310] However, most organization consider ethical and moral behavior as driving forces toward productivity.[311] Organizations have "ethical standards, a group of professional processes guidelines or codes for doing what is deemed the right practice."[312] However, ethics can vary among organizations,[313] but it is standardized with the governing boards. If an individual does not adhere to the ethics standards, written guidelines, or core values within the organization, this lack of adherence "can impact the organization reputation and finances."[314]

Say Askew et al., "The three most important precursors of unethical behavior are the individuals, the ethical issues itself, and the organizational culture."[315] An individual with a lack of moral values can have an impactful decision-making process,

---

[309] Octavia A. Askew, Jeffrey M. Beister, and Jetonga Keel, "Current Trends Of Unethical Behavior Within Organizations," *International Journal Of Management & Information Systems (Online)* (2015): 107.
[310] Ibid.
[311] Ibid.
[312] Ibid.
[313] Ibid,
[314] Ibid., 108.
[315] Ibid.

provoking unethical choices in the workplace.[316] In fact, "individuals who portray behavior or action that reflect negative characteristics are considered to be more prone to behavior that is wrong."[317] To manage some of the unethical behaviors in the workplace, organizations provide a code of conduct or ethics.[318] This code of conduct underlines what the organization seeks to uphold in terms of personal communication, model behavior, and generally agreed upon class.[319] Leaders must understand "that how a person under their authority is treated will dictate their actions and behaviors."[320] Leaders are held to a higher standard; they live under a microscope both personally and professionally. Their words and actions are judged according to others' perspectives, like it or not. They must be ready to give an account of their behaviors in the workplace.

Since leaders can set the tone for an atmosphere, they must demonstrate a positive attitude around others. There is nothing worse than working with a negative person for eight hours of a day; it is emotionally and physically draining. If the person is leading others, everyone else under that leader will become negative as well, causing an unproductive culture—a ripple effect. Negative behavior is contagious, and it spreads so fast throughout an organization. Unethical behavior can be contagious as well, "spreading through relationships between perpetrators and observers lead to similar attitudes towards unethical behavior."[321]

In fact, people with similar thought processes tend to

---

[316] Ibid.
[317] Ibid.
[318] Ibid., 109.
[319] Askew, Beister, and Keel, 109.
[320] Ibid
[321] Franziska Zuber, "Spread of Unethical Behavior in Organizations: A Dynamic Social Network Perspective," *Journal of Business Ethics* (2015): 152.

interact more together, supporting unethical or ethical behaviors. Unethical behavior needs to be examined to keep it from spreading and creating a culture of accepting wrong behaviors.[322] Cote goes so far as to argue, "Unethical behaviors create a toxic work environment resulting in negative consequences that affect organizational goals and tasks, organizational resources, motivation, employee morale, and job satisfaction."[323] And the headship of sinking ships—leaders who cut down their peers and followers—cause lasting damage for those around them.[324] It is a "dark side of leadership" that has plagued our society.[325] "While good leaders place ethics at the core of leadership," warns Cote, "bad leaders tend to follow unethical behaviors, hurt people and cause destructive outcomes in organizations."[326]

Unethical behavior was a familiar scene with Linda's boss. Linda recalled an employee wanting to celebrate her team members during the annual professional week. The employee decided to consult Linda's boss about the activities surrounding the event. Linda's boss gave the employee permission to host the event, even though it was not his idea. The employee was told to be creative with the event, making sure it would be successful. The employee spent numerous hours seeking donations from her colleagues for the event, and Linda's team was supportive, giving extra time to help with the event. The employee wanted to give her leaders and team members a gift, a small token of appreciation. She had collected numerous pens, flashlights, staplers, and other work-related tools to give away; the gifts presented no extra costs for the area. The employee was so excited about her accomplishment prior to the deadline.

---

[322] Ibid.
[323] Robert Cote, "Dark Side Leaders: Are Their Intentions Benign or Toxic?" *Journal of Leadership, Accountability, and Ethics* (2018): 43.
[324] Ibid.
[325] Ibid.
[326] Cote, 43.

However, Linda's boss had been persuaded by his friends on the leadership team that the employee had done something wrong. Linda was told that the employee did not follow protocol in gathering the tokens of appreciation. Linda replied, "What do you mean? She asked for permission, and it was granted to her." Linda's boss asked Linda if she had the gifts in her possession.

Linda replied, "No."

Linda's boss and his friends began to search the office space they occupied for boxes. The boxes were not there, so Linda's boss called the employee to get the boxes. Linda met with her employee at a later date to discuss the matter. The employee was screaming and crying. The employee told Linda that the boss gave her a verbal warning for collecting donations among her colleagues. The boss requested that all the donations be turned into his office. Linda was upset about an act of kindness being destroyed for no reason other than pride. Linda's boss could not let his friends be wrong, so he was willing to hurt the employee. Linda encouraged her employee, and she gave her recognition for caring about the team. As the professional week approached, Linda's boss gave all the same gifts to the team members, including one to the employee, as tokens of appreciation.

Wow! Linda could not understand how that was ethical. If the boss felt it was wrong for the employee to give the gifts, it should have been wrong for him to distribute them. Linda's team members heard about the incident, and they were visibly upset. They refused to accept the gifts from the boss, but he did not care. Linda had a group discussion about the matter, allowing them to express their thoughts and concerns. The employees' opinions backed up a general rule in leadership theory: employees seek leaders who behave morally and stick to their values, proving they can withstand the test of time.[327]

---

[327] Cote, 43.

Linda's team began to question the behavior of their boss. However, the distraught employee could not get beyond the incident, and she eventually resigned. While Linda did not agree with the outcome, she respected and understood the employee's decision. The employee's husband did not want her to continue to work under the boss's authority. Linda had a discussion with her boss, but he never apologized for the incident. Sometimes leaders miss the mark in leadership, but they must be willing to admit it and face the consequences.

■   ■   ■

Another incident where Linda's boss behavior was questioned occurred when Linda was acting as a lead for the shift. She had made the assignments out equally among the team members, but one of the team members refused to accept his workload. Linda did not have a supervisor to report the incident; instead, she called the boss of the entire team to let him know about the situation. Linda explained the situation to the boss, and the boss became annoyed about being called on the weekend.

He asked her, "Why are you calling me?"

He said, "I am not in town, and I cannot help you."

Linda said, "I just need a little advice about the employee refusing to take his assignment."

Linda was not prepared for the words that had come out of the boss's mouth.

He yelled, "If you don't like your job, you can find another one."

Linda did not understand what the comments had to do with the situation. She replied, "What?"

The boss repeated himself, "If you don't like your job, you can find another one."

Linda was shocked at the boss's comments, and she did not receive any direction about the situation. Linda politely thank him for his time, and she decided to end the phone conversation.

Linda decided to tell the employee if he did not want to take the assignment, he could go home. The employee decided to take the assignment, and things worked out for Linda's team. The boss denied his behavior, even though others witnessed the conversation on both ends of the phone. Sometimes leaders must face opposition for the betterment of the team.

Personal Struggles

Leaders are facing many obstacles in turbulent times. When leaders are dealing with personal struggles, it can create challenges for them in leadership. "Everyone has that one personal struggle," admits Bostick.[328] Most of the time, "leaders are demand-led and anything can cause them to be acute."[329] However, it is the maturity of the leader that determines how to respond when life is shaking the foundation of their leadership. Some leaders can hold on during the shaking, and some leaders cannot endure. Personal struggles can cripple leaders' movement if they are not supported in a healthy manner. Personal struggles are not meant to destroy an individual but to strengthen them as leaders. The best advice comes from those who have been there and experienced life as a leader. Leaders who can manage their personal struggles are highly effective in managing issues in the workplace. In fact, "personal struggles are often prerequisites to doing something significant in life and in business."[330] The truly great leaders may overcome struggles out of public view, but in those private times, they still enjoy enormous growth.[331]

---

[328] Jacqueline Bostick, "'Everyone Has That One Personal Struggle' Video," *McClatchy-Tribune Business News* (2013).

[329] Stuart Handysides, "My Struggles with Personal Development," *GP* (2004): 21.

[330] Stephen R. Covey, "Unifying Leadership," *Executive Excellence* (1999): 4.

[331] Ibid.

Linda had her share of personal struggles on the leadership journey. Linda found herself falling in love with another employee within the organization. He was a perfect fit for Linda's life and treated Linda like she was a queen. He was in a leadership role when they eventually became engaged. They began to read the policy about relationships among leaders and followers within the organization. They even sought advice from Linda's boss. He replied, "It should be okay."

Linda was so happy about the engagement. Immediately after the wedding, though, Linda's new husband was demanded to change positions and leave his leadership role. Linda's spouse eventually lost his job. However, Linda refused to allow the negative incident to impact her view of leadership. It was a personal struggle that she had to overcome. Linda continued to abide by the organization's core values with a great attitude. She loved working for the organization.

As the years went by, Linda had to deal with another personal struggle, having to receive surgery on her hand while taking sign language for a bachelor's degree. Linda had to take time off from work until she was released from the doctor. While out on the medical leave, Linda's mother began to develop medical problems and eventually died as a result of postoperative complications. Linda had to plan the funeral with her siblings. One of Linda's sons could not attend the services since he was out to sea with the US Navy. After the funeral, Linda had to return to work as a leader and listen to others' health struggles with their loved ones. Linda had to overcome the memory of losing a loved one. Linda's personal struggle gave her a measuring rod to use in life—nothing could measure up to losing her mom. Linda used the rod to help others. Linda utilized her faith, the support of friends and family as a stepping stone to keep moving forward in life.

Summary: Building Block Six

During turbulent times, leaders face many struggles within organizations and their communities. Change and challenges are constant in leadership. It is part of reaching objectives and becoming successful in life. Some challenges in leadership arise through work-life balance struggles, fears and failures, competition, missed opportunities, knowing and doing the right thing, and unethical behaviors in leaders. However, these are common encounters, and with the right assistance, leaders can overcome them. Every leader deals with some form of struggle in their personal or professional life. Even great leaders had to experience great failures to obtain great success. Quitting is not an option for effective leaders. They change direction if things are not working while learning from mistakes along the pathway to the destination of leadership. Challenges will make a leader wiser, stronger, and more effective.

Chapter 7

Diversity in Leadership

One of Linda's friends frequently provided Christmas gifts to a group of coworkers. Each year, Linda and her friends eagerly waited for the gift, knowing they would get the best present. The friend enjoyed shopping and decorating her home during the Christmas season; every year, her living room was changed into a winter wonderland for guests. The friend gave the same present to each person. She usually passed them out when she was working with them. However, one year, Linda's friend asked her to pass out the gifts. Linda was willing to assist her friend with a simple task. Linda's friend gave her a total of three gifts including one for herself. The gifts did not have any names on them, but it really was not required since all of them were the same size with the same wrapping paper. Linda gave the first gift to one of the people on the list.

However, the next day, Linda gave the second gift to the other person. Linda left her gift in the trunk of her car. She usually opened it on Christmas day. When Linda gave the second person the gift, the friend decided to open it in Linda's presence. As she unwrapped the gift, both of them had known it was something beautiful. The gift was a beautiful African American angel.

Linda said, "I think that might be my gift."

The friend said, "Why do you think that, Linda?"

"I am not sure, but let me go to my car and get my gift."

Linda went down to her car for the gift and returned with the gift to open in front of her friend. Linda unwrapped the gift, and it was a beautiful Caucasian angel. They both began to laugh. What did this mean? It was a hilarious moment in the hallway for them. Linda indeed had given the wrong gift to her friend, and Linda had the wrong gift, according to the gifter. They said, "What are we going to do about this?" while still laughing.

Linda said, "We are going to keep the angels that we currently have in our hands."

They could not stop laughing at the mistake. Linda and her friend's relationship was deeper than their ethnicity. It was based on their love for each other, and until that defining moment, they had not seen ethnicity among them. Linda and her friend had to face their differences, and they did so with joy and love. It was not a mistake after all, but it was a test of their unconscious biases. They made the decision to place the angels on their fireplace mantels and to reflect on the unexpected moment of laughter. Linda had to call the friend who purchased the beautiful gifts and tells her about the mistake. Linda apologized to her for mixing up the gifts, even though they were not labeled. Linda told her about their decision not to exchange the gift, but the friend was not happy about Linda's mistake. In fact, she never asked Linda to do the simple task again. Somehow, "people need to come to terms with diversity."[332]

---

[332] Patricia Digh, "Coming to Terms with Diversity," *HR Magazine* (1998): 117.

Diversity

Organizations are filled with many people from different backgrounds working together for common goals. The differences provide a uniqueness among them, shaping a diverse organizational culture. "Diversity," says Patricia Digh, "can be viewed as a comprehensive leadership process for developing an atmosphere that works for all employees. It is all the ways in which people are similar and all the ways in which people are different,"[333] and it is not wrong. Diversity entails many areas in the workplace such as "gender, age, values, work style, emotional intelligence, geography, skills and more."[334] There are benefits in having a diverse group of people; "it can provide advantages in the form of new ideas and different knowledge sets."[335] However, "when leaders listen and accept others input before injecting their opinions, it can make a difference."[336] Creating a culture of diversity takes courage, effort, and an understanding of the importance of its influence, starting with leaders.

In fact, "organizations with a diverse culture tend to have different goals, management styles, decision-making processes, and systems that cause a need for standardized competencies for managing diversity."[337] While teams that cultivate diversity enjoy the strength of "forming and storming," they need to be properly led to the "norming and performing phase."[338] However, "it takes leadership

---

[333] Ibid.

[334] Terrie Temkin, "Diversity, Diversity, Everyone Wants Diversity," *Nonprofit World* (2009): 6.

[335] Anonymous, "Diversity Is Not Diversity Is Not Diversity," *INSEAD Articles* (2008).

[336] Ibid.

[337] Jan Visagie, Herman Linde, and Werner Havenga, "Leadership Competencies for Managing Diversity," *Managing Global Transitions* (2011): 227.

[338] Janice L. Dreachslin, "The Role of Leadership In Creating A Diversity-Sensitive Organization," *Journal of Healthcare Management* (2007): 152.

commitment and employees' buy-in to successfully launch a diversity initiative."[339] Organizations' culture appearance should mimic their surrounding communities. "Diversity must become integrated into incentive plans, strategic plans, performance management process, and new employee orientation, and it must become an important factor when assessing employees' opinion," warns Gail Warden.[340] Thompson adds, "If organizations are not going to be inclusive as possible, they will not be successful in employee's engagement."[341]

Fear of Diversity

Diversity must not be feared.[342] In fact, the leadership team should create a culture of fearlessness.[343] It is easy to interact with people, places, and things who fall within an individual's comfort zone. It does require effort to interact with somebody and some things that are different, but it is meaningful in the long run. Differences have been around from the beginning of time, and they will continue to be part of our society and organizations.

What does a person gain if he or she is willing to work only with those who appear to be similar to them? Why are some people afraid to approach diversity? These questions require more awareness and dialogue. In fact, the apostle Paul made human differences known; he declared, "Welcome one another as Christ has welcomed you, for the

---

[339] Ibid.
[340] Gail Warden, "Leadership Diversity," *Journal of Healthcare Management* (1999): 422.
[341] Pam Thompson, "Leadership Diversity: The Path to Value-Based Care," *Hospital and Health Networks* (2015): 43.
[342] Anonymous, "Fear of Diversity," *Wall Street Journal Europe Brussels* (1994): 8.
[343] Suarez, 8.

glory of God."[344] People are unique, and Paul affirmed this truth many times.

However, some people are afraid as a result of the lack of knowledge about diversity. They have a negative reaction out of a deeper inner fear about others who are different from them in age, gender, ethnicity, culture, beliefs, values, religion, work ethics, and leadership style. Interacting with others from a fear stance only makes the organizational culture worse; it can add chaos to chaos. Fear of failure and of change can become distracting and hindering for organizations and workers.[345] "It destroys trust and quality of work life, and it is a barrier to better outcomes," insists Suarez.[346]

However, it takes courage to overcome the fear of diversity.[347] MacGibbon emphasizes that, in answer to fear, leaders must remember that "courage is not the lack of fear—it is resistance to fear."[348] Courage is born when individuals realize that they must fight against the poison of fear.[349] It takes a strategy to conquer the fear. MacGibbon continues, "It starts with facing the fear, establishing a purpose that is greater than fear and staying present in the moment."[350] The atmosphere needs specific factors for employees to deal with their fears.[351] Suarez declares, "The right leadership, trust, and vision are needed to create a fearless culture."[352] Having these factors can "develop win-win dynamics" for diversity to be accepted among people and employees.[353]

---

[344] Roman15:7 (English Standard Version).
[345] Gerald J. Suarez, "Managing Fear," *Excellence* (1996): 8.
[346] Ibid.
[347] Marti MacGibbon, "Never Give Into Fear," *SuperVision* (2011): 9.
[348] Ibid.
[349] Ibid.
[350] Ibid., 10.
[351] Ibid.
[352] Suarez, 8.
[353] Ibid.

Dr. Sharon E. Downey, DSL

Managing Diversity

Linda had started working a second job for the clinical experience and extra income. She had heard about the organization through word of mouth. Linda was enthusiastic about working with a different population of patients, ranging from children to older adults. Linda was extroverted in personality; she worked well with anyone, always speaking with her colleagues. One of Linda's colleagues at the second job gave her some insight as a new therapist in the profession. He was a seasoned therapist. He told Linda in a casual tone, "You have two strikes against you. One, you are an African American. Two, you are a female." As a fairly new professional, Linda was interested in learning from seasoned therapists. She listened to their perspective and believed that it held value. Linda could not believe the comments, since the other professional did not even know her.

However, the colleague's comments could not be ignored; it was an integral part of Linda's life. People do not get to choose who they are and how they look in life, but they do get a chance to choose what they can do with their lives. Based on the colleague's comments, Linda had a feeling that her journey would not be an easy one in the profession, but she was ready for the challenges. Linda continued working for the organization, making new lasting relationships with different people.

Earnest and Shawnta Friday note victoriously, "Many organizations have created and implemented various types of programs in an effort to deal with diversity."[354] In fact, if diversity is not properly managed, it can affect the bottom line of a business.[355] Organizations who have cultures that value

---

[354] Earnest Friday and Shawnta Friday, "Managing Diversity Using a Strategic Planned Change Approach," *The Journal of Management Development* (2003): 863.
[355] Ibid., 865.

diversity are most likely successful in managing diversity. [356] Maxwell et al. encourage the development of more of these programs by emphasizing that "the management of the differences among employees can be an asset to work being done more efficiently and effectively."[357] Indeed, add Epting et al., "managing diversity can improve communication among employees, reduce bias toward nontraditional employees, orient all employees to an organizational culture that values diversity, and meet the needs of all groups of employees."[358] However, "programs to manage diversity are most effective when senior management is accountable for program implementation and delivery."[359] Any diversity program must consist of the following:

- ☐ Assessing the organizational culture for current behaviors and attitudes towards diversity
- ☐ Creating clear objectives and goals for the diversity program
- ☐ Communicating effectively the vision of the diversity program
- ☐ Monitoring the progress of the diversity program, ensuring the goals are being met [360]

James Rogers insists that "organizations must make managing diversity as an essential part of their overall quality strategy if they are to succeed"[361] and the organization is to main-

---

[356] Ibid.
[357] Gillian A. Maxwell, Sharon Blair, and Marilyn McDougall, "Edging towards Managing Diversity in Practice," *Employee Relations* (2001): 469.
[358] Laurie Ashmore Epting, Saundra H. Glover, and Suzan D. Boyd, "The Health Care Supervisor," (1994): 73.
[359] Barbara Ettorre, "Diversity: Managing Diversity for Competitive Advantage," *Management Review* (1993): 6.
[360] James O. Rodgers, "Implementing a Diversity Strategy," *LIMRA'S MarketFacts* (1993): 26.
[361] Ibid

tain a competitive advantage over its competitors. As stated before, "managing diversity requires strong and consistent leadership as well as educational programs for all groups of employees."[362] Also, "it requires a strategy where accountability, rewards systems, and market analysis are incorporated."[363] Leaders and their followers have a part in diversity, but the ultimate responsibility for its success is dependent upon leadership.

Stereotyping

Does being different equate to being wrong? Being different does not, but judging others to be inferior or suspect due to their differences certainly is.[364] Society needs to move from stereotyping others based on their appearance. Instead, they must learn to look at people as just that—people—without looking first to stereotypes they can force upon a person.[365] In fact, "stereotyping is always morally wrong."[366] However, "there are connotations that come with every organization, but stereotyping people just because they are in a certain organization is based on unfair judgment and impression."[367] Stereotyping stops people from forming meaningful "connections" and working relationships: it hinders teamwork.[368] It cripples people from reaching their fullest capacity within organizations. While stereotyping is often frowned upon, it still

---

[362] Rodgers, 26.
[363] Ibid.
[364] Erin Beeghly, "What Is a Stereotype? What Is Stereotyping?" *Hypatia* (2015): 675.
[365] Anonymous 5, "See the Person, Not the Stereotype," *Southern Gazette* (2009): 3.
[366] Beeghly, 675.
[367] Zach Melusen, "Opinion: Stereotyping Organizations Leads to Unfair Judgment," *University Wire* (2018).
[368] Ibid.

exists both consciously and unconsciously within societies and organizations. People are not saying it, but their actions are reflecting it in their communities and organizations. Effective leaders should not have a "judge the book by the cover" mindset. After all, it really is about understanding diversity.

Who are the people in the workforce?

There are different generations of people that are supporting the operations of successful organizations. The workforce can consist of traditionalists, baby boomers, and members of Generation X and Generation Y (or millennials). Their collaboration in knowledge and skills keeps the flow moving in the right direction. No organization can survive with only one generation of people; it will be short-lived. Who are the generations performing behind the walls of organizations in the twenty-first century? Do they appreciate the diversity among them? Are they intimidated by the diversity among them? Every generation has a role to play in organizations, fitting together in the bigger picture and culture as a whole.

Traditionalists

Francis-Smith begins a description of traditionalist workers by noting that "they were born before 1946, grew up during difficult times in society; the Great Depression and two world wars plagued their communities."[369] They were dependent upon radio for communication and entertainment during family time.[370] Traditionalists are known for their dedication and service to their country.[371] They perform well in organizations

---

[369] Janice Francis-Smith, "Surviving and Thriving in the Multigenerational Workplace," *Journal Record* (2004): 1.
[370] Ibid.
[371] Ibid.

with leadership utilizing a "command-and-control structure."[372] Traditionalists are dependable employees.[373] They know organizational culture well from decades of experience in the same.[374] They are mindful of waste, and they do not like people who are rude in nature.[375] "They usually do not question authority" and are very respectful employees.[376] Traditionalists are set in their own ways. "They usually do not have multiple employers in their lifetime."[377] Some of them are trying to adapt to the rise of technology, but "many are struggling due to technological illiteracy."[378]

Linda had a diverse team with a few traditionalists. Linda had employees that refused to change along with technology, both in their work and personal life. While making routine daily rounds with staff members, Linda noticed that one of the team members was using a phone. As Linda approached her, Linda realized the team member had a flip phone. The team member was so proud of her phone, bragging about the cost of her bill. It was extremely cheap, and the phone was paid in full. Linda asked if she could send or receive text messages on the flip phone. Of course, the answer was no. The phone looked outdated, but the team member was comfortable using it to make calls. No picture-taking or checking emails with the flip phone. The team member always dressed professionally in a pressed long white lab coat. She was an on the job trainer (OJT), and she was waived from some of the past job requirements.

However, it was a matter of time before technology in the workplace would impact her life. The organization upgraded

---

[372] Ibid.
[373] Ibid.
[374] Alison Simons, "Changing Workplace Demographics: T+B+Y+X=Opportunity," *CPA Practice Management Forum* (2009): 15.
[375] Francis-Smith, 1.
[376] Simon, 15.
[377] Ibid.
[378] Francis-Smith, 1.

its reporting system, and all the employees had to be educated and make adjustments in their learning style. The employees were given a new upgraded phone to use as part of their work tools. It was their personal work phone for sharing information; it would only work on campus. Linda knew that the team member would most likely struggle with the new phone since it involved sending and receiving messages among different disciplines. Linda prepared the traditionalist ahead of time through conversations about the changes to come with the phones.

In fact, Linda even allowed the traditionalist to practice on her phone since it was the same phone that the organization had purchased. The traditionalist struggled at first but with much coaching, understanding, patience, and usage, she was able to adapt to the new processes. Linda asked the traditionalist if she would ever purchase a new personal phone, and the answer was still no, even though she really liked the new phone. Knowing and identifying possible diversity issues prepared Linda and the team member for a smoother transition.

Baby Boomers

"Baby Boomers," notes Francis-Smith, "are born between 1946 and 1964 and are children of the traditionalists."[379] They represent what Simons calls "world changers."[380] It was during this generation that more women began to work outside the home, adding to the family income.[381] "Baby Boomers are extremely loyal to their employer, and they adopted behaviors from their parents," adds Simons.[382] They are work focused.[383]

---

[379] Francis-Smith, 1.
[380] Simons, 15.
[381] Ibid.
[382] Ibid.
[383] Ibid.

"Baby Boomers are usually optimistic in heart and they have the faith to change the organizational culture."[384] Baby boomers are involved in the well-being of their elderly parents.[385] They work well in chaos, but they prefer things to be in order.[386] Baby boomers have seen many changes in the workforce, and they usually worked several jobs simultaneously.

In addition, the family is important for them. Some of them are providing full-time care for their grandchildren. Simons reminds leaders that "Baby boomers are faced with managing their time and money during times of uncertainties."[387] They are resourceful employees. They are more informed and concerned about changes in their organization and staying in alignment with policies and procedures. Additionally, they always come to work prepared and are respectful to those in leadership roles, regardless of the leader's age. As far as their leaders, Baby boomers respond best to "consensus management."[388] They take pride in their appearance and performance. They are confident, competitive in the workplace, hard workers, and award-driven.[389] Notes Francis-Smith, "They do not like laziness and authoritarianism, but they are known to micro-manage people."[390] "They usually have more work-life balance … [and] tend to be idealistic and are willing to sacrifice personally and professionally in order to be successful," Kapoor and Solomon argue.[391] The retirement phase is usually in sight for them. As a result of unforeseen circumstances, some baby boomers are working beyond retirement years.

---

[384] Ibid.
[385] Ibid.
[386] Ibid.
[387] Ibid.
[388] Francis-Smith, 1.
[389] Ibid.
[390] Ibid.
[391] Camille Kapoor and Nicole Solomon, "Understanding and Managing Generational Differences in the Workplace," *Worldwide Hospitality and Tourism Themes* (2011): 309.

Therefore, organizations must understand the value of baby boomers and find ways to benefit for their human capital.

Generation X

Generation X arose between 1965 and 1980, and their shaping was influenced deeply by uncertainty as they saw parents "facing hardship and increasing personal debts, witnessing challenges to the honesty of national leaders, and recognizing the threat of AIDS in their personal relationships." Francis-Smith describes them as "children who witnessed America's failures."[392] Additionally, "they are known as latch-key people for letting themselves into the house after school since both parents were working."[393],[394] However, note Kapoor and Solomon,

> They are independent, self-reliant, and unsure about leadership They rather work alone instead of working on teams; they can struggle with undeveloped interpersonal skills. However, they are an asset to a team, bringing their "multi-tasking" skill set. ... They are good at overseeing simultaneous projects as long as they have control in managing the direction of them. Work-life balance is more important to them, and they will not sacrifice their personal life for the organization.[395]

Adds Simons, "They are not naturally collaborative, but rather proud of their self-reliance and independence; they

---

[392] Francis-Smith, 1.
[393] Simons, 15.
[394] Kapoor and Solomon, 309.
[395] Ibid., 309–310.

expect to get recognition for their contribution to the team."[396] In fact, "they place a low value on loyalty to a specific employer or keeping regular work hours. ... They love change, freedom, and room to grow, and are educated enough to move into management a lot sooner than the Traditionalists and Baby Boomers. ... The leadership structure they work well with is based on competence."[397] "They do not expect to work in the same organization for a lifetime," says Simons.[398]

Linda had enjoyed her diverse team, but it did not fall short of its challenges. Whenever there is a group of people in the same setting, there is a chance for disharmony to exist. Linda recalled one employee from Generation X who was flexible with her schedule, but she was never really committed to the team or organization. It often reflected in her time with others. She did not want to have anything to do with teamwork. She wanted help when it was needed, but she rarely offered help to others. The employee worked on an as-needed basis for the organization. The employee wanted to travel around the world, and she did it throughout the year. The employee was asked to work a specific shift, and she replied, "I cannot work. I am in China." The employee had never given her time to help the team unless it supported her personal travels. Linda understood that the employee loved the autonomy of working according to her own schedule. Most of the time, members of Generation X would rather work alone, and they are independent employees.

Generation Y or Millennials

"Millennials," explains Francis-Smith, "are born between 1981 and 2000; they are just beginning to enter the workplace."[399]

---

[396] Simons, 15.
[397] Francis-Smith, 1.
[398] Simons, 15.
[399] Francis-Smith, 1.

They are called tech kids, " being born into a world of advanced technology, and learned to mastered technology at such a young age, developing skills for multi-tasking."[400] Kapoor and Solomon describe this generation as becoming more wealthy, technology savvy, educated, and full of ethnically diverse members when compared to previous generations.[401] They understand the changes in technology, possessing the most recent smartphones and other wireless devices.[402] They often communicate with others through the internet and social media, creating a belief in an instantaneous nature of communication reached only in modern times.[403] Unfortunately, add Kapoor and Solomon, "They are known to have poor communication and problem-solving skills."[404] Francis-Smith also notes that millennials are an upbeat generation, preferring optimism over what they see as the negativity of older generations.[405] They are outgoing and adventurous[406] and honor authority figures in their lives.[407]

In addition, "They prefer an inclusive style of management."[408] They have an immediate mindset, wanting to know things now.[409] Millennials desire communicative leaders—those who will share how they are doing[410] and are great team players.[411] However, they would rather have room to perform the tasks in their own way as long as the goals are reached.[412]

---

[400] Ibid.
[401] Kapoor and Solomon, 310.
[402] Ibid.
[403] Ibid.
[404] Ibid.
[405] Francis-Smith,1.
[406] Ibid.
[407] Ibid.
[408] Ibid.
[409] Francis-Smith,1.
[410] Ibid.
[411] Kapoor and Solomon,310.
[412] Ibid.

Millennials are often misunderstood: their quickness and comfort with technology can come across to traditionalists and baby boomers as "know-it-all" traits. Leaders must spend time learning from them as well as learning about them; it can be a rewarding opportunity.

That was the case with Linda: she had a project to orchestrate with the purpose of creating a culture of safety for her team. Linda's team had expressed concerns about not being allowed to make a mistake or speak up without it being frowned upon. Linda wanted to change her team's perspective. Linda created a core group of team members to launch the safety project. The core team had a millennial, baby boomers, and members of Generation X as a representation of the whole team. Linda wanted input from all generations since different perspectives can eliminate groupthink from brainstorming sessions. Linda had used a whiteboard to write the vision and their mission, the plan to execute, and its deadline. Linda had given the core team sticky notes to write their ideas to place on the whiteboard. The session was productive, with everyone providing feedback on defining the root of the problem. The whiteboard was covered with sticky notes, arranged methodically to outline the complete plan. Linda realized time was running out—she had to stop the session so she could capture all the information. It was difficult to facilitate and take notes at the same time.

Linda needed some help from a team member and asked a millennial to copy the notes from the whiteboard while she continued to dismiss the group. The millennial agreed but said, "I will use my phone to take a picture of the board and send it to your email."

"What?" Linda replied. "What kind of phone do you have?"

The millennial had a smartphone. Linda had not heard of the process before working with the millennial: using a phone to send notes. Linda was so impressed with the technique that she went and purchased a smartphone that same day. Linda had learned something valuable—millennials enjoy showing older generations new technology devices. Linda's job became easier as a result of the millennial's expertise with technology. Linda never had to write a note from another meeting; she just used her phone. Linda relied upon the millennial to keep her abreast of the latest trends in technology, and it worked. Technology can be a conversation starter for leaders who struggle with members of Generation X and millennials in the workplace.

Therefore, traditionalists, baby boomers, members of Generation X, and millennials all must work collaboratively within organizations. Their behaviors are not wrong; they are just different. When you take the differences and add them together, the sum becomes "opportunities," or optimal outcomes.[413] Diversity is a chance to make things better for all groups of employees. However, taking courses on diversity and having discussions about diversity is not enough for twenty-first-century organizations. It is time to practice diversity until we get it right. Why? Because the workforce has a variety of people ranging from young veterans with post-traumatic stress disorder (PTSD) to aging employees and different genders. We can no longer turn our heads, hoping the differences will go away. We must respect the differences of others as we expect for them to respect our differences. Scripture supports this position: "Jesus declared, 'So whatever you wish that others would do to you, do also to them, for this is the Law and the Prophets.'"[414] It is the Golden Rule for our society, and it must become part of the twenty-first-century organization's core values. What would happen in our organizations if we treated others how we expected to be treated? What does a Golden Rule organizational culture look like?

---

[413] Simons, 23.
[414] Mathew 7:12 (English Standard Version).

Summary: Building Block Seven

Organizations are operated with different groups of people from all walks of life with different beliefs and foundations. Leaders are confronted with diversity daily in the business sector, and they need insight on how to have openness to others' views and input for engagement and decision-making purposes. Diversity is not a wrong thing, but it is a different thing. Diverse teams are more productive; they add value to an organization. People tend to become fearful of the unknown, but fear of diversity must be removed within organizations. Diversity must be respected. Leaders must have an understanding of how to manage diversity and must understand the implications of allowing stereotyping within their organization's culture. The workforce consists of the traditionalists, baby boomers, and members of Generation X and Generation Y (or millennials). Each group of people contributes to a successful workplace by learning, sharing information, and working toward a common vision.

Chapter 8

Faith in Leadership

Faith Is

Is faith a requirement for leadership? Most leaders practice faith in either their ethical or unethical behaviors. The scriptures declared, "Now faith is the assurance of things hoped for, the conviction of things not seen."[415] Robert Hoerber noted, "In faith, things hoped for become realized, or in faith, things hoped for becoming reality."[416] Faith is, in essence, the simply yet powerful belief in something.[417] The phrase "keep the faith" is often heard in difficult times[418]—this phrase is meant to give an individual hope when things are moving the opposite direction in life.[419] Baker notes that the author of Hebrews specifically intended the eleventh chapter as an

---

[415] Hebrews 11:1 (English Standard Version).
[416] Robert G. Hoerber, "On The Translation of Hebrews 11:1," *Concordia Journal* (1995): 78.
[417] Kimberly F. Baker, "Hebrews 11—The Promise of Faith," *Review and Expositor* (1997): 440.
[418] Ibid., 439.
[419] Ibid.

encouragement for those believers who needed to keep the faith.[420] The early Church leadership and followership faced many trials as a result of their faith,[421] but Hebrews 11 remained a bastion of hope and a plea to remain courageous.[422] "Faith gave the substance to their hopes and it convinced them of the realities they did not see," adds Baker. "It is a characteristic of the Christian life which makes it possible for people to endure hardship because they have the conviction of the reality of the unseen world."[423]

Moreover, "faith is active, it hopes, obeys and it moves out in trust."[424] The scripture declared, "What good is it, my brothers, if someone says he has faith but does not have works?"[425] Faith requires movement in order for it to be measured and effective. In reference to this and other passsages of James, Sharyn Dowd insists that "James denies that faith and works are separable, insisting that a life characterized by works of mercy is proven to have faith, whereas the claim to have faith apart from having works is unproven and therefore empty."[426] However, everyone is subject to understanding. Newbigh argues, "Faith is not a substitute for knowledge, but it is the only way to knowledge."[427] Newbigh poses the question: Is it possible to gain true knowledge without having faith in some unknowns?[428] Yet, the degree to which a person believes is totally dependent upon self-willingness. "A person's faith will be stronger or weaker to the extent that the person is willing

---

[420] Ibid.
[421] Ibid.
[422] Ibid.
[423] Ibid., 440.
[424] Ibid.
[425] James 2:14 (English Standard Version).
[426] Sharyn E. Dowd, "Faith That Works: James 2:14–26," *Review and Expositor* (2000): 198.
[427] Lesslie Newbigh, "Certain Faith: What Kind of Certainty?" *Tyndale Bulletin* (1993): 340.
[428] Ibid.

to take greater or lesser risks in situations," argues Michael Pace.[429] Also, "the strength of a person's faith is seen when they are taking risks without being fearful."[430] People are different, and their "strength of faith" level will vary.[431]

Jesus often challenged others in their belief. He would remind them of having no faith or little faith, but he made clear that faith was necessary for things to come. The death of Lazarus demonstrated this test of faith. The scriptures declared,

> Now when Jesus came, he found that Lazarus had already been in the tomb four days. Bethany was near Jerusalem, about two miles off, and many of the Jews had come to Martha and Mary to console them concerning their brother. So when Martha heard that Jesus was coming, she went and met him, but Mary remained seated in the house. Martha said to Jesus, "Lord, if you had been here, my brother would not have died. But even now I know that whatever you ask from God, God will give you." Jesus said to her, "Your brother will rise again."[432]

Mary and Martha believed in Christ's leadership. He was known as their teacher who performed many miracles. Yet, even in Jesus's absence, Mary and Martha had faith in his effectiveness. They had known the outcome would be different under Jesus's authority; all he had to do was speak the word in their situation. John Warnek reminds readers that "Mary and Martha awaited and saw the miracle of life with their

---

[429] Michael Pace, "The Strength of Faith and Trust," *International Journal for Philosophy of Religion* (2017): 149.
[430] Ibid.
[431] Ibid.
[432] John 11:17–23 (*English Standard Version*).

brother, Lazarus."[433] After performing the miracle of bodily resurrection, "Jesus said to Martha, did I not tell you that if you believed you would see the glory of God?"[434] Jesus used the opportunity to develop the faith of those around him. "Faith like that of Mary and Martha is not blind and ignorant," says Warnek. "They knew Jesus' power and goodness."[435] They had faith in their leader's ability to make things happen. His words were the final authority in their lives, and they accepted his leadership. Jesus's authenticity to his followers made their faith stronger. He was an ethical leader, setting the pathway for leaders to follow. Christ's leadership was about serving others in the community. When leaders are demonstrating ethical behaviors, people will believe in their mission.

The Shaping of Linda's Worldview

Faith can impact a person's worldview. Stiffney argues that "worldview is more than just a fuzzy philosophy. In its richest sense, it is about how we view reality and how it shapes the way we live."[436] Worldview is the groundwork for a leader—it forms a foundation, which built upon turns into morality and value, and subsequently informs how leaders behave.[437] "A leader," Stiffney warns, "can shape the moral character of the organization and its service and place in the larger society."[438] Therefore, faith must be part of their personal values. Faith is a powerful leadership tool. How can leaders get others to buy into an idea if they do not believe in it themselves?

---

[433] Jon Warnek, "In Midst of Suffering, Christ Is There," *The Billings Gazette* (2017).
[434] John 11:40 (English Standard Version).
[435] Warnek.
[436] Rick Stiffney, "Leadership as Landscaping," *The Journal of Applied Christian Leadership*: 97.
[437] Stiffney, 97.
[438] Ibid.

A Leadership Strategy

For many years, Linda had faith in God. She knew that her life was centered on her faith and family. Yet, Linda was respectful to the worldview of others. Linda had taken a biblical course for a bachelor's degree. The college was founded on Christian principles. Linda had assumed that all her classmates were of the Christian faith, but she really did not know. The professor introduced himself as being a person who did not believe in God. He apologized if he offended anyone, but he wanted to let them know. He thought of himself as solving the world's problems with a group of friends around the table without spirituality, and he was proud of his position in life. Linda's class was given an assignment that required them to give an individual presentation. Linda and her classmates prepared for the assignments; they were supportive of each other. However, Linda's classmates were careful in the mentioning of their faith. No one mentioned their personal faith prior to Linda's turn. Linda stood before the group of students and her professor and began to talk about what the scriptures declared: "Live in harmony with one another. Do not be haughty, but associate with the lowly. Never be wise in your own sight."[439] Paul challenged believers to practice a non-violent approach in evil times.[440] Michael Barram reminds readers that Paul's non-violent behaviors, "when they are exercised, undermined the tendency toward the human self-interest that produced violence."[441]

Linda was expounding on the topic, and her classmates concurred with her research. Linda completed the presentation by taking questions from the group. The professor asked the first question: "Linda, do you view the world through Christianity?"

Linda was astonished and afraid at the same time. Linda knew that her grade was dependent upon on her answer. After

---

[439] Roman 12:16 (*English Standard Version*).
[440] Michael D. Barram, "Romans 12:9–21," *Interpretation* (2003): 425.
[441] Ibid.

all, a professor who did not share the same faith was risky business when it came to analyzing the scriptures. The class was quiet, waiting to hear Linda's response.

Linda took a deep breath and answered the professor. "Yes, I believe in Jesus Christ. I have accepted him as my personal Lord and Savior." Linda told the group that Christ died on the cross for her sins and that he rose from the grave. She emphasized that she had asked Christ to forgive her for her sins and that salvation was free to all that believed. Linda talked about Christ being her lifestyle and how her worldview was shaped through him. The professor did not say anything else, and Linda went to her seat. Linda was trembling as she sat there trying to figure out why he asked her that life-changing question.

However, Linda knew she had to take a stand for her faith. Linda noticed that the atmosphere changed after her presentation. Her classmates began to mention their faith along with scriptures. The evening became an opportunity to shape others' worldviews, even the professor's. Linda and her classmates talked about the opportunity after class. They were pleased with the outcome. Linda went home, not sure if she would get a fair grade, but she was not overly concerned. She did not denounce her faith in front of others, and that was more valuable.

Vocation

How does an individual view their work? "Is it just a job or a vocation?"[442] The answers to these questions will position a person for fulfillment in their work, bringing meaning to their labor. The scriptures declare, "Only let each person lead the life that the Lord has assigned to him, and to which God has called him."[443] "Vocation is another word for purpose or call-

---

[442] Mike Broad, "Tough Choices for a Vocation," *Hospital Doctor* (2005): 2.
[443] 1 Corinthians 7:17 (English Standard Version).

ing," explains Gene Veith.[444] God decides which assignments are given to people.[445] Drawn to the Lord, saved individuals receive gifts and talents that assist in their work for God's kingdom.[446] In this way, God is at work on the earth to redeem what has been lost to sin and to honor the righteous.[447] Yet, no leader gets to choose their vocation. "They do not decide what their vocation is; they receive it," says Wheatley.[448] It might be the opposite of their desires, but it will find them. Wheatley declares, "The notion of vocation describes work that is given to us, that we are meant to do."[449]

■   ■   ■

However, "leaders' work can give them more than a vocation by causing them to realize their potential, and their engagement in satisfying and more productive work."[450] When the purpose is present in leadership, people's lives will be impacted in the marketplace. And years of observation on human nature confirm that "most people yearn to experience a sense of purpose in their lives."[451] Wheatley even argues that a sense of purpose and vocation deeply affects leadership charisma. He claims, "The stronger a leader's sense of vocation, the more resilient and courageous he or she appears to be."[452] Vocation prompts leaders to "make

---

[444] Gene Edward Veith, "Vocation: The theology of the Christian life," *Journal of Markets and Morality*, (2011): 120.
[445] Ibid.
[446] Veith, 120.
[447] Ibid.
[448] Margaret J. Wheatley, "Spiritual Leadership," *Executive Excellence* (2002): 5.
[449] Ibid.
[450] Anonymous 6, "Job Gives Them More Than Vocation," *Gulf News* (2007): 1.
[451] Wheatley, 5.
[452] Ibid.

things better, and create an atmosphere of stability" for their employees.[453] Leaders gain great courage and timeless wisdom when they fall into step with what they are called to do.[454] Workers are magnetized to those leaders who develop strong personal values and stick to them, even through difficult situations.[455] Additionally, "leaders who adopt their vocation portray service, passion and fit within organizations."[456] They are aligned with the needs of others.[457] They operate in their faith.

For instance, Linda had often seen her profession as a job in the earlier days of her career. She worked two different jobs for extra income for her family. Linda rarely called off for a scheduled shift; she was a dependable employee. She had become dedicated to helping others who needed it within the organization, regardless of their profession or title—if they needed help, Linda would provide the service. If Linda did not have the answer, she would find the answer for them. Linda enjoyed helping others; it was a natural characteristic of hers.

However, Linda knew that her love for the work made it more than a profession. It had become a vocation. The turning point came after Linda received an education in leadership. Her work gave her a bigger sense of fulfillment, and people's lives were being changed as a result of her vocation. In the midst of Linda's work, spiritual therapy was intertwined. She always looked for the needs of others, trying to reduce discomfort and painful moments in people's lives. One evening, while making rounds, Linda witnessed a new employee crying. Linda saw others consoling the employee,

---

[453] Ibid.
[454] Richard J. Leider, "The Leader In Midlife," *Business Strategy Series* (2008): 115.
[455] Ibid.
[456] Ibid.
[457] Ibid., 116.

and Linda was immediately drawn to the incident. Linda kept her distance until the right moment came around. Linda cautiously approached the situation and asked the employee if she was okay; then the employee began to tell Linda her life story.

The employee had been engaged to get married, but her fiance decided to end the relationship. Linda's heart sunk within her as she listened to the sadness of a beautiful person. Linda had to do something to make it better for her. Linda and the employee shared the same faith, and they had read the same inspirational book. It was because of these connections that Linda and the employee's relationship developed. The employee's life got better, and Linda was able to move on searching for others with needs. Linda realized that her vocation brought peace to her work life as a leader.

Wisdom

Scripture declares,

> Who is wise and understanding among you? By his good conduct let him show his work in the meekness of wisdom. But if you have bitter jealousy and selfish ambition in your hearts, do not boast and be false to the truth. This is not the wisdom that comes from above, but it is earthly, unspiritual, demonic. For where jealousy and selfish ambition exist, there will be disorder and every vile practice. But the wisdom from above is first pure, then peaceable, gentle, open to reason, full of mercy and good fruits, impartial and sincere. And a harvest of righteousness is sown in peace by those who make peace.[458]

---

[458] James 3:13–18 (English Standard Version).

If someone is considered wise, it usually alludes to the fact that she or he is educated or cognitively advanced.[459] In the book of James, wisdom is seen as something that can be acted upon and observed objectively.[460] Wisdom, to the author of James, means literal moral choices between right and wrong, or between God's will for one's life and the opposite of His will.[461] Wisdom from above is a free choice: "only the fool sense no need for wisdom."[462] But although wisdom can be freely chosen, cautions James's author, it is a vital necessity in the day-to-day.[463] The book informs Christians on how to pursue wisdom and cultivate, eventually finishing with the discernible products of wise action.[464] "Wisdom is not a human achievement, says Perkins. "It comes by the faith of the individual who is seeking it. James makes a comparison of wisdom from above and wisdom of society.[465] Perkins adds to the discussion, noting that many individuals assume they know how the world will react and get wrapped up in preparing for the best and worst vocational outcomes, eventually experiencing failure and disillusionment.[466] Wisdom provides the strength to endure hardship in life, and "it enables us to face life's tests and live through them consistently making the right decisions and having insight into the purposes and the will of God."[467] Also, "wisdom has a significant impact on success and impact at the individual, organizational and community levels."[468] "Wisdom is seen as contributing to effective strate-

---

[459] David W. Perkins, "The Wisdom We Need: James 1:5–8,3;13–18," *The Theological Educator* (1986): 17.
[460] Ibid.
[461] Ibid.
[462] Ibid.
[463] Ibid.
[464] Ibid.
[465] Ibid.
[466] Perkins, 19.
[467] Ibid., 23.
[468] Jennifer Rowley, "What Do We Know about Wisdom?" *Management Decision* (2006): 1247.

gic decision-making and to the interpersonal processes crucial to effective leadership," says Jennifer Rowley.[469] "It informs the visioning required of leaders, the use and content of the dialogue, and the maintenance of the psychological contracts between leaders and followers."[470]

* * *

Linda's life was driven by wisdom from above. She utilized wisdom to make daily choices in life. However, when Linda did not consult the wisdom from above, she paid an immense price in the long run. Once, Linda found herself in the middle of two employees' altercation. The first employee claimed that the other one was mean towards her during an event. Linda was reluctant to intervene since she had noticed that both employees were best friends at some point in time. Linda asked the first employee to speak with the other employee since they shared a ride to work. The first employee claimed that they no longer shared a ride, and she was uncomfortable speaking with the other employee. At the sound of that, Linda had to get involved since the employee felt some discomfort about the situation. Before proceeding, Linda asked for wisdom from above, and she eventually discovered that the first employee had lied about the entire incident, causing disharmony among team members.

Accountability

Leaders of faith are held to a higher standard, but all leaders must be accountable for their actions. Does this mean anything in our society? Everyone has an opinion of others' wrong and right behaviors, but they do not look at their own

---
[469] Ibid., 1250.
[470] Ibid.

behaviors. Accountability must first start with self or the image in the mirror—how could you judge someone else's flaws and faults without addressing yourself? "A truly accountable leader knows what it means to be a leader; they are not waiting to get permission to get the job done, insists Molinaro."[471] "An accountable leader is fully committed to moving things forward in their organization and takes full and personal ownership for their words and actions."[472] And, he adds, "lame leadership" results when there is no oversight or cooperation between leaders and those who lead them in turn.[473] In fact, "unaccountable or mediocre leaders often go through the motions and pay lip service to business strategy."[474] They manage to deceive others around them, undermining people and operating with a hidden agenda to advance themselves, but they will get caught. Who are these leaders? Leaders display confidence in and care of the people under them when they understand that they must be looked over themselves.[475] Rose Patton says, "Leaders must take accountability for ethical leadership and never become complacent that they are safe from the failure of ethical leadership"[476]—a failure can suddenly happen.

Linda had seen her share of leadership woes, and she often questioned, "How did that incident occur with that person?" She believed that leaders' hidden behaviors will surface in crisis moments in their personal and work life. The pressures of leadership squeeze them, and they respond either positively or negatively to others. Linda had observed a new leader who

---

[471] Vince Molinaro, "Driving Leadership Accountability: A Critical Business Priority for HR Leaders," *People and Strategy*: 32.
[472] Ibid., 33.
[473] Ibid.
[474] Ibid., 36.
[475] Ibid.
[476] Rose M. Patten, "Link People, Strategy, And Performance," *Executive Excellence* (2003): 20.

began to become disrespectful toward everyone on their level or below their level. At first, Linda thought it had something to do with the excitement of the new leadership role, but the behavior began to intensify and people began to whisper about the individual. She thought that the leader's superior needed to enroll them in a leadership development program, since it is impossible to become a successful leader without structured developmental training. Linda recalled being in a meeting with the individual, and it was an unprofessional scene. They were blaming everyone except themselves for unforeseeable circumstances. Linda thought maybe the leader was dealing with personal issues, as that type of situation was common for them. However, Linda later found out that the leader was operating from a position of insecurity; they had a low self-esteem issue, which prompted fears within to surface. The leader undermined and undercut everyone who threatened their progress to their promised destination, even Linda. This situation showed Linda that personal accountability is essential. "The people at the top set the tone, key values, and standards," says Paton.[477] "Without personal accountability at the top, anything can go on in the ranks below."[478]

Success

Those with wholeness in all areas of their personal and work life are symbols of true success. Success goes beyond making money and participating in a materialistic lifestyle, only to boast about things that have rusted or no longer exist. Success is defined differently by different people.[479] Kirkwood says, "It can be seen as the accomplishment of one's goals, or attainment

---

[477] Patten, 20.
[478] Ibid.
[479] Jodyanne Jane Kirkwood, "How Women and Men Business Owners Perceive Success," *International Journal of Entrepreneurial* (2016): 594.

of wealth and prestige, fame, position, social status, or honors. People's meaning of success is directly connected to their decision-making in education, employment, relationships, and life satisfaction."[480] Some people in society glamourize success, living in every second of the day to acquire a taste of it. Some people will go to the extreme in achieving success, especially within organizations. Climbing the corporate ladder prompts people to do things that are deemed unethical, but are ethical within their mindset. Kirkwood reminds readers that "For organizations, success has traditionally been measured in terms of financial success."[481] Organizations provide products and services to increase the bottom line, differentiating and giving them a competitive advantage in the industry.

However, leaders must learn how to obtain success in the right manner. First of all, "leaders need to develop self-confidence."[482] It is impossible to reach a goal without visualizing the end of the goal. Leaders must see the end from the beginning of the process. "Mental visualization can be powerful."[483] Leaders must also have a strong inner knowledge of their abilities. Leaders must focus on those abilities, and not someone else. Leaders can only be good at being themselves; they should not try to be another leader. Self-confidence requires practice, stepping out in faith until it built. Also, a leader must "become a positive thinker. Leaders can think positively or negatively. It is a choice."[484]

"However," says Cohen, "most negative people do not expect positive results. They live with the worst expectancy, and it happens."[485] The mindset paves the way for productivity in a person's life. It is a simplistic perspective and approach.

---

[480] Kirkwood, 594.
[481] Ibid.
[482] William Cohen, "Climbing The Ladder of Success," *Personal Excellence Essentials* (2018).
[483] Ibid.
[484] Ibid.
[485] Ibid.

If leaders think that things will not work, then it will not work. If leaders think they can conquer and reach all goals, then it will happen.

Lastly, "leaders need to be enthusiastic about everything. If leaders are not excited about something, no one else will be. Leaders cannot expect others to enthusiastically accept a challenge that they have not enthusiastically accept themselves."[486] The change will always force leaders to respond, but they do not have to be doubtful, negative, or unimpressed about it. Leaders need to stop complaining and just do the work with a good attitude.

The scriptures say:

> As they went on their way, Jesus entered a village. And a woman named Martha welcomed him into her house. And she had a sister called Mary, who sat at the Lord's feet and listened to his teaching. But Martha was distracted with much serving. And she went up to him and said, "Lord, do you not care that my sister has left me to serve alone? Tell her then to help me." But the Lord answered her, "Martha, Martha, you are anxious and troubled about many things, but one thing is necessary. Mary has chosen the good portion, which will not be taken away from her."[487]

The story gives insight into the leadership and followership among the Lord and the sisters. Geoff New says of Jesus's rebuke of Martha, "It makes one wrestle with and confronts the negative effect of claiming that one's busyness is so important that attentiveness to Jesus is considered inferior."[488]

---

[486] Cohen.
[487] Luke 10:38–42 (English Standard Version).
[488] Geoff New, "The Voice: From Text to Life-The One Thing," *Stimulus* (2014): 33.

"Martha's name means "sovereign lady" or "ruling lady."[489] New continues,

> Her work is described by the Greek word *diakonia*, which is used positively elsewhere in New Testament, but the spirit of her expression of *diakonia* was anything but positive. Martha who speaks was silenced by Jesus. Mary, who is silent, is spoken for by Jesus.[490]

Martha was unsuccessful in the interaction.[491] However, Jesus made it known that success—or the most important thing in serving others—had been found by Mary. Kilgallen notes that "it was the listening, or hearing, the word that will not be taken from her."[492]

Servant Leadership

Robert Greenleaf coined the phrase "servant leadership" and began to expound on how he defined it.[493] Greenleaf served as vice president of AT&T, studied organizational leadership extensively, and performed as a leadership consultant to many large corporations.[494] "Servant leadership is based on the idea of serving other clients, employees, customers, or the community as the first priority," Carrol says.[495]

---

[489] Ibid., 34.
[490] Ibid.
[491] Ibid.
[492] John J. Kilgallen, "Martha and Mary: Why at Luke 10:38–42?" *Biblica* (2003): 555.
[493] William J. Byron and Tom Gallagher, "The Church Can Learn a Lot from 'Servant Leadership,'" *National Catholic Reporter* (2010): 26.
[494] Ibid.
[495] Archie B. Carroll, "Servant Leadership: An Ideal for Nonprofit Organizations," *Nonprofit World* (2005): 18.

He continues:

> Leaders have two responsibilities: they must be concerned with performing tasks and concerned with helping people. However, servant leaders are concentrated first on helping people. Servant leaders begin by wanting to serve and then come forward with the desire to lead. It is a natural position that is often taken, serving others. According to Greenleaf, servant leadership begins with the natural feeling that one wants to serve, to serve first. Servant leaders do not look for a return reward in serving others; it is seen as a privilege to serve. This kind of person is distinctively different from one who is a leader first, perhaps because of a desire for recognition, name, power, and money.[496]

They are not self-serving leaders or leaders through self-ambitions. Some business organizations are taking on the model of servant leadership.

However, "it is one thing to speak of the aspirations to serve others, but how does it translate into practice?"[497] It starts with "adopting a servant leadership" mindset within the culture.[498] "It requires incorporating servant leadership into the board education."[499] Who are the board members serving?" asks Carroll.[500] "It requires integrating servant leadership into community leadership organizations,"[501] developing a partnership with them. In addition, "leaders can use servant leadership

---

[496] Ibid.
[497] Carroll, 19.
[498] Ibid., 20.
[499] Ibid.
[500] Ibid.
[501] Ibid.

in education or learning by doing."[502] "Organizations can offer servant leadership courses as part of management education and training," Carroll recommends.[503] Also, "organizations can apply servant leadership principles in personal-growth programs."[504]

Servant leadership is a basic concept to utilize. It is a helping-others-first mindset. However, it requires humility for its effectiveness. If a leader expects to gain much outwardly from serving others, then she or he will be disappointed in their work. Servant leadership is inwardly compensated; people's lives are changed through serving. Linda had a love for her team. She was a servant leader, and she accepted her leadership style. Linda had a natural ability to serve others. Linda worked during the holidays so others could spend time with their families, and she often willingly spent personal funds to support her team's activities. Being a servant leader caused Linda to daily examine herself before serving others. Linda had to make sure the reason for serving and the purpose of serving others remained unselfish as a leader. Linda had to ensure her heart was in the right condition for serving others with no hidden motives. "For the LORD sees not as man sees: man looks on the outward appearance, but the LORD looks on the heart."[505] Linda knew that she was being held to higher accountability.

Linda in the Making

Leadership development is enduring. Linda had more progress to make in becoming a servant leader. She was far from perfecting leadership as a whole, but she was moving in the

---

[502] Ibid.
[503] Ibid.
[504] Ibid.
[505] 1 Samuel 16:7 (English Standard Version).

A Leadership Strategy

right direction. Linda had developed an attitude of acceptance to change itself both personally and professionally. She could not prevent it from coming, and she knew things were going to happen. However, the change would make her wiser and stronger. The scripture declared that "She dresses her with strength and makes her arm strong."[506] When leaders cease to change or cease adapting to change, they stop growing in the midst of it all. Linda faced many hardships both personally and professionally, but she was still standing tall. Linda contributed the triumphs to faith, family, and true friends. Her personal philosophy was 'always be true to yourself and be true to others.' As the scripture declares, "Her children rise up and call her blessed."[507]

Linda spent the majority of her life serving others, and only at the end of the day did she work on her personal needs. "If we all applied God's revealed wisdom to our domestic lives, I cannot think but that our children will rise up and call us blessed."[508] Linda prayed that God would use her life to show his love, and he did it throughout her travels. Linda never met a stranger on the journey—only people who God loved. God's Word says, "Charm is deceitful, and beauty is vain, but a woman who fears the Lord is to be praised."[509] "It is universally true that a person who fears Yahweh is to be praised."[510] The scripture declares, "Many women have done excellently, but you surpass them all."[511] Linda's life had become a testimony to God's goodness, God's mercy, and God's grace. Hers was a life that was dedicated to serving others in the church, community, and at work.

---

[506] Proverbs 31:17 (English Standard Version).
[507] Proverbs 31:28 (English Standard Version).
[508] Jana K. Riess, "The Woman Worth: Impression of Proverbs 31:10–31," *Dialogue* (1997): 151.
[509] Proverbs 31:30 (English Standard Version).
[510] Riess, 151.
[511] Proverbs 31:29 (English Standard Version).

Summary: Building Block Eight

All leaders have a belief system. Faith is believing in something unseen and usually shapes a person's worldview or perspective. Linda, for example, explained the steps in accepting Christ as her personal Lord and Savior to others. Faith allows an individual to view their work as a vocation, giving a stronger meaning to the tasks and their responsibilities. Wisdom from above is priceless, and it is essential for leadership. All leaders must be held accountable for their behaviors inside and outside organizations. Unaccountable leaders can negatively impact an organization's business plan. Successful leaders are those with completeness in both their personal and professional life. Servant leaders are those with an others-first mindset. Businesses are using a servant leadership model for their employees. The making of a good leader is supported through faith.

Chapter 9

Pearls of Leadership

Whether leadership is viewed as a position or process, it produces fruitful benefits in the lives of leaders. There are pearls of leadership. One anonymous author noted,

> The very mention of the word pearls call up a range of glorious images, from classic to the contemporary. Pearls symbolize Hollywood glamor. Pearls symbolize high style. ... Pearls symbolize simple elegance. They are the only gems produced by a living creature. A natural pearl is formed when an oyster cannot expel a parasite or piece of sand that has entered its body. Pearls are royal favorites. Pearls symbolize wealth and opulence. Pearls are beautiful. Authentic pearls are valuable. Pearls are precious and delicate gems. Pearls symbolize timelessness. Individuals should understand that these treasures from the sea require special care. Pearls offer variety. Pearls symbolize professionalism.[512]

---

[512] Anonymous, "A Few Pearls of Wisdom," *JCK* (2003): 200–205.

Sarah Shannon, on the plundering and use of pearls in antiquity, notes, "It was not uncommon for a captain to be murdered for one and be thrown overboard by [a] greedy crew."[513]

However, in leadership, pearls are produced as lasting relationships, networking, development, growth of self and others, the return of investment in employees and their families, love and support from employees, trustworthy employees, faithfulness to the vision, honor, and respect as a leader. Leaders have a chance to make leadership whatever they want it to become and reap its rewards. The Bible declares, "Do not be deceived: God is not mocked, for whatever one sows, that will he also reap."[514] In this passage, says Staggs, "Paul's warning is not that God will punish those who violate his laws, but that his laws operate universally and inevitably. What one sows one reaps, in human existence as in gardening."[515] The harvest is a result of the planting of seeds. "What you sow is what you reap: What you see is what you get; the chickens have come home to roost," Johnson reminds leaders.[516] With leadership, the concept is similar, the good seeds planted in the lives of others will produce a harvest of pearls.

Harvest Time

For instance, Linda had planted numerous good seeds along the way on her leadership journey. Linda believed in seedtime and harvest time as a leader. Linda never had a dull moment at work. There were so many needs that had to be met. She made sure employees had a sympathy card when a loved one passed; she purchased cards to match their situations and

---

[513] Sarah Shannon, "The Long Fall and Curious Rise of the Pearl Industry," *FT.com* (2017).
[514] Galatians 6:7 (English Standard Version).
[515] Frank Stagg, "Galatians 6:7–10," *Review and Expositor* (1991): 248.
[516] Earl S. Johnson Jr., "Galatians 6:1–10," *Interpretation* (2000): 302.

A Leadership Strategy

she ensured that other team members signed the card; she purchased small gifts for team members as a token of recognition and thanksgiving. Linda reaped everything that she had sown into the lives of others. Linda was given a new office, and the staff decided to decorate her office space with gifts from them. Linda's team made a picture with all of them on it, calling themselves her work family. Routinely, Linda found cards, notes, and words of encouragement on her desk when she needed it the most. One of Linda's employees pasted the phrase "be amazing today" on the wall in Linda's office space.

One day, Linda decided to purchase donuts with her personal funds for her team and other departments, giving them out as a token of teamwork. After Linda had finished distributing donuts, she was having a conversation with another employee who gave her a free fundraiser coupon with twelve buy-one-get-one-free dozen donuts from the same store used by Linda. She was able to purchase more donuts in the future for others. It does not matter what is being sown; the reaping is equally the same. Harvest time is the best time in leadership work.

Lasting Relationships

Working closely with people allows for professional relationship development to occur between leaders, employees, and others around them. "When it comes to forming those key long-term relationships, quality is many times more important than quantity," Currin states.[517] "The opportunities for relationship building can occur naturally" in healthcare.[518] Toward creating those quality relationships, Carrie Matthew reminds

---

[517] Darren Currin, "Commentary: Lot Lines: Building Relationships," *Journal Record* (2008).
[518] Carrie Mathews, *Forging Ties: How to Build Solid Relationships* (CIO Canada, 2007).

readers, "The most important part of the relationship building process is finding the right person to cultivate."[519] Everyone is not a candidate for a lasting relationship, so leaders must approach it with cautiousness. There must be some earned equity within an individual for the relationship to grow into a lasting one.

Matthew continues, "Relationship building requires credibility and trust."[520]

Linda's Lasting Relationships—In Life and Death

After being in the profession for many years, Linda had seen many employees enter and leave the profession and the organization for personal reasons. Linda believed in supporting employees' future pathways. Linda had one employee who wanted to change organizations for a benefit reason. The employee wanted to do something different, getting a change in pace and a closer drive to home. The employee left the organization but remained in contact with Linda. They saw each other as Linda was moonlighting with the other organization. The former employee was pleased with her decision, making relationships in the new culture. One day, at the end of Linda's shift, the former employee wanted to speak with Linda. She wanted to share personal information. It was at that moment that Linda realized that their relationship had trust—the former employee trusted Linda. The former employee had faced some health challenges, but she was strong throughout them. Linda remained prayerful for the former employee.

Several years later, the former employee developed more health challenges, and she quietly passed away at home surrounded by her family and friends. Linda had supported her and the family until the end. Linda's mother and the former

---

[519] Ibid.
[520] Ibid.

employee both were laid to rest in the same garden of remembrance. Linda continued to support the family, keeping in touch with her daughters. Whenever Linda visited her mother's gravesite, she made sure to visit the former employee as well, sometimes dividing her flowers among them.

Linda's Lasting Relationships—
In the Past and the Future

Linda cared deeply about her staff, and she had no regrets, spending each moment as if things could unexpectedly change in the next moment. Linda never wasted her time in leading them; she wanted the best for their personal and work life. Linda had an employee who wanted to move his family away; there were better prospects for his spouse in another state. The former employee made a decision to support his entire family, and it worked well for them. The former employee was a humble man, always giving to others for the good of the community. He dedicated his life to making sure his spouse thrived in her new leadership role, and their children excelled in school and after-school activities. Linda made sure he had the proper tools to make the change in state licensure required for the profession.

The former employee kept in touch with Linda, updating on the family's progress. In fact, they did not sell their home, so they were required to return occasionally. The former employee and his family experienced success in all areas of their lives. They helped so many within the community, not expecting anything in return. A few years later, Linda had to attend graduation in the same city where the former employee relocated. Linda sent them an invitation, and the former employee called and accept the request. The former employee's spouse made preparations for Linda's visit. She created a detailed agenda for Linda's stay. They picked up Linda from the airport and made sure she checked in at the hotel.

Although Linda did not have any family members in that city, the former employee and his family made Linda's graduation day special. They made sure Linda did some tourist activities, so she had the best time with the family. At dinner, the children prayed for Linda's life, asking God to bless her in school and at work. Linda had experienced God's love on another level as she witnessed the prayers of the children. The scripture declares, "Whoever humbles himself like this child is the greatest in the kingdom of heaven."[521] In response to this statement of Jesus's, Don Garlington reminds Christians, "This was the point of comparison with the disciples; Instead of making 'grown-up' demands, they must become like children, and embrace powerlessness and a low profile."[522]

Networking

Leadership presents chances for networking to materialize. "Networking is a set of goal-directed and motivation-driven behaviors," says Huang.[523] It enhances an individual's leadership progress.[524] Huang adds, "Effective leaders understand the necessity of networking in organizations."[525] Even though networking done well is an encouragement and a helping hand for both parties involved, networking not done in the correct way can end with frustration, mutual disdain, and career stagnation.[526] Toward finding the proper networking relationships for you, Lenz reminds leaders, "Success depends on building

---

[521] Mathew 18:4 (*English Standard Version*).
[522] Don B. Garlington, 'Who Is The Greatest?' *Journal of the Evangeli Theological* (2010): 293.
[523] Yin-Mei Huang, "Networking Behavior: From Goal Orientation To Promotabilty, *Personnel Review* (2016): 907.
[524] Ibid.
[525] Ibid.
[526] Anna Navarro, "Good Networking/Bad Networking," *Physician Executive* (2011): 60.

and sustaining a range of relationships within and outside the organization."[527]

Linda's Networking

To illustrate, Linda was allowed to work with a local external non-profit organization to promote lung health within the community. The organization held an annual team event for stair climbing. Linda was part of the committee. She met with other business leaders once a month to strategize in fundraising for their team and the nonprofit organization. Linda met a lot of people over the four years. It gave Linda insight into offered community services. Linda's employer had provided funding to the organization in addition to their team's contribution, so she had a chance to learn from other leaders, sharing in their decision-making process. Linda's input was respected, representing her employer with an attitude of professionalism. Linda continued to network. She had to compete in raising funds and finishing the event. Linda had a strategy for her team. The event was held at a company that had forty-two flights of stairs. However, Linda had never climbed a large number of stairs in her life; it was a battle in her mind that she had to win. Linda had to practice along with the other leaders to prepare for the event. There was only one way out of the staircase since the other entrances were purposely blocked. Participants had to climb the stairs and used the elevators to get back down to the first floor. Linda had to create a team with people willing to climb stairs. The aim was to promote better health and their profession in the community at the same time. Linda had always felt socially responsible for her community. Linda created the organization's first team for the stair climbing event. She and her climb team held pep rallies to get buy-in from other employees.

---

[527] Thomas Lenz, "Networking As A Leadership Habit," *Public Administration* (2013): 364.

Linda's team held garage sales for fundraising. They participated in the fundraising activities held by the non-for-profit organization, such as holding a silent auction and partnering with a local restaurant to serve customers.

On the day of the event, Linda and her team were ready to climb to the top of the building. Linda started cheering with her team to motivate them in the presence of their competitors. The teams were sent into the staircase a few seconds apart, one member at a time, ready, set, and go. Linda went into the staircase last, making sure she supported and watched the takeoff of her team members. Since there were forty-two flights, Linda had to make small goals to finish the climb. She had to climb in multiples of tens, then she had to celebrate. Linda continued the strategy until she reached the finish line. People were lining the staircase to encourage participants in keeping moving forward. As Linda climbed the last flight of stairs, she had a burst of energy; the end was nearer than the beginning. Linda's mind kept her moving even though her body wanted to stop: her legs were beginning to ache. Linda did it, finishing the climb of forty-two flights of stairs in twenty-eight minutes. Linda's team members finished in ten to fifteen minutes. They met the fundraising goals with the nonprofit organization. The event was a huge success for her team. Afterward, Linda continued to maintain her relationship with the external organization.

Lenz finishes his discussion by emphasizing, "Networking is used to find leaders, to find allies, to raise money, and to acquire expertise and ideas."[528]

Growth and Development in Self

Linda's life had changed as a result of seeking to be a better leader. She went through a phase of growth and development.

---

[528] Lenz, 364.

Linda did not understand some of the challenges in her life, but she kept the faith and believed that God had a great plan for her life. Linda had to learn about the meaning of leadership and its place in her life. She had to face the failures in leadership as a result of making mistakes and use them as a building block to becoming a better leader. However, Linda also had to examine herself and address any hidden issues that kept her from moving forward. Linda was told by a leader within the organization that she would complain when she was given more work.

However, while Linda did not concur with the findings, Linda decided to use the feedback as a goal for the upcoming year. Linda wrote out the information on a sticky note not to complain about additional responsibilities, and she attached it to her personal computer as a constant reminder that she must master this ability. Linda wanted to excel in her work performance, but it required continuous learning and experience in leadership. Linda had enrolled in high education for leadership. While Linda did not become a charge nurse, she did become a leader in healthcare. Linda had grown in her personal life, and adversity had made her stronger and wiser. Linda had known that transformation really started with the person in the mirror—an irreplaceable pearl.

Growth and Development in Others

Investing in others' growth and development is beneficial for the employee and the organization. They become human capital, which is valuable within organizations. Overell explains, "Human capital is the stock of assets that we have as individuals."[529] It allows employees to acquire skills and knowledge for their personal usage and career pathway. Overell continues,

---

[529] Stephen Overell, "You Should Reap What You Sow," *Personnel Today* (2005): 13.

"Employees rent out their human capital to employers in exchange for the usual benefits, such as reward, affirmation, and development."[530] Employees are not staying in the same job for decades anymore due to a new generation with a technology mindset. However, "learning and development are associated with commitment, and it is still one of the most likely sources of positive responses from employees."[531]

For example, Linda made a conscientious effort to invest in her staff through career planning. It was part of the annual appraisal process. Linda met with an employee who had a desire to work in another field in healthcare. Linda asked the employee if she could partner with him to pursue his goal. The employee welcomed Linda's assistance. In the future, Linda invited the employee to a lecture on lung disease. A visiting physician was speaking on the topic. After the lecture, the employee expressed an interest in pursuing the topic. Linda and the employee mapped out the course to reach his goal. The employee had to do some research on the requirements for the future position. He had to take coursework and gain certification in the desired area. The employee contacted the physician for more information, developing a relationship with him. The employee had become stagnant in his current role, so he desperately needed a change.

Leaders need to understand that when employees come to the point of having a lack of interest in their work, it is time to make an adjustment in their work life. Linda met with the employee to get an update on his status. The employee had become involved in projects throughout the organization. As a result of the right connections, the employee had his contribution published in the finished project. Linda helped the employee transfer to another department, whereupon

---

[530] Ibid.
[531] Todd J. Maurer and Michael Lippstrey, "Who Will Be Committed to an Organization That Provides Support for Employee Development," *The Journal of Management Development* (2008): 342.

he reached his goals and his final destination. The employee was happy and satisfied with the transition. It was a job well done.

Respect and Honor

In light of the leader's requirements to respect those under them, Kirsch asks, "What is the virtue we most urgently need more in America today?" [532] This is a time where people are calling wrong behaviors the right behaviors and people are calling right behaviors the wrong behaviors. Organizations' cultures are built on their core values, such as respect and honor. "To be honorable is to be brave, committed, and self-sacrificing;"[533] "it means living by a code, and putting the group before the individual."[534] Luis Lopez defines honor as an objective and outwardly-viewed symbol of goodness known in a society.[535] He emphasizes that while externalities can never strip away symbols of honor that are earned; one who enjoys honorable titles can lose the titles for themselves.[536] However, Lopez reminds leaders, "serve others with respect and integrity and no one will ever question your honor."[537]

For instance, Linda's leadership style—servant leadership—allowed her to place others' needs before her own. Linda always looked for ways to make things better for her team. She never requested anything from them in return and served her staff around the clock. Linda called her team in the middle of the night since they worked in healthcare, checking for possible needs. Linda cried with her staff, she

---

[532] Adam Kirsch, "Does Honor Matter?" *Yerepouni Daily News* (2018).
[533] Ibid.
[534] Ibid.
[535] Luis Lopez, "Honorable Life Is a Goal for Us All," *Tampa Tribune* (2008): 2.
[536] Ibid.
[537] Ibid.

laughed with them, she listened to their struggles, she provided advice when it was requested, and she loved them. Linda's team supported her in return; they would perform any tasks that she asked them to do. Linda thus had influence over the team. Linda cared about each team member and their families, and some of them cared about Linda. Some of the team members decided to nominate Linda for an organizational service award, an award given to an individual with distinctive behaviors in serving others. Linda was thrilled to be nominated for such a service award, but her direct boss did not support the nomination, and she did not win.

However, a few years later, Linda was nominated a second time. Linda was grateful for the consideration in her work life. Linda's team wanted to thank her for the services to them. Linda remained humble, as her work was always done unto the Lord. Linda could not cut corners or take a short cut in her job performance. Linda honored the Lord in both her personal and professional life. Linda thought that her direct boss would be on board with the second nomination: after all, she had faithfully served him. Linda had soon found out that he decided to nominate another person, causing her not to win again. Even though Linda lost twice, she did appreciate the moments of respect and honor from her team.

Making a Difference

There is nothing better in leadership than making a difference in the lives of others, creating a change for the better, and being a witness to the difference. "Every now and then someone comes along who makes a tremendous difference in our lives," Whatley declares.[538] Yet, we all as "individuals

---

[538] Cathy Whatley, "Leadership: Making A Difference," *Executive Speeches* (2003): 34.

have the power to make things happen, to get things done, and to connect with our communities."[539] Though scholarship is important, Jeffrey Glazer reminds leadership scholars that "it is important for leaders to spend less time talking about what leadership is or is not and spend more time trying to improve their community."[540] There are so many needs within our communities, and it takes everyone doing their part together to bring about change. However, within organizations, leaders can make a lasting impact. It requires them to focus more on the things that are going well, with the intent of fixing the things that are not going well. The change will always produce problems, and there should be a level of acceptance to the issues; it gives leaders a chance to make a difference.

A Sense of Accomplishment

"You did it!"

How many times have you heard that phrase? How many times have you told yourself, "You made it?" Well, leading others gives you a chance to have that experience. Leadership allows individuals to set personal goals and accomplish them. Leadership is really personal: it tears you down, then rebuilds you into the right image. Success comes when there is a sense of accomplishment in the life of a person.[541] Success, then, say Ashar and Lane-Maher, "is a balance of life and work."[542] Sarah Barmack notes that, in the lives of employees in general, accomplishment is felt

---

[539] Ibid.

[540] Jeffrey Glazer, "The Call for Leadership," *Journal Of Leadership Studies* (1995): 111.

[541] Hanna Ashar and Maureen Lane-Maher, "Success and Spirituality in the New Business Paradigm," *Journal of Management Inquiry* (2004): 255.

[542] Ibid.

both when specific goals are recognized and when employees understand how those goals help the company reach its big-picture goals.[543]

For instance, Linda had experienced a sense of accomplishments throughout her life. She had beaten the odds that society had placed on her life after being told that she was limited in both her personal and work life. The scripture declares, "I can do all things through him who strengthens me."[544] Linda believed in the scriptures. They were like an anchor in the sea, keeping her in place as she tossed and turned in life. Linda had become an effective leader. She had learned how to produce the best outcomes as a leader. Linda was amazed at her life, and her achievement of four degrees with another one in the making. The scripture declares, "This is the LORD's doing; it is marvelous in our eyes."[545]

Linda could not take any credit for the results in her life. She understood that God has known the plan of her life from the beginning, and she had to trust him that it would turn out for his best. She understood that having a strategy or planning is a major part of our everyday living beyond leadership. Even though Linda made some wrong choices that took her off the right path and made the journey longer, Linda did find purpose, finish the course, and reach her destination in life. She told everyone, "When it comes to a leadership strategy, I have been there and done that!"

---

[543] Sarah Barmak, "Building a Better Worker," *Maclean's* (2013): 62.
[544] Philippians 4:13 (English Standard Version).
[545] Psalm 118:23 (English Standard Version).

Summary: Building Block Nine

Leadership is a reaping moment regardless of the difference in the stance taken by leaders. Leadership produces pearls, beautiful and professional looking. Leadership is beneficial and rewarding to those involved in the process. Some of the benefits are harvest time, building lasting relationships, networking, earning respect and honor, making a difference in the lives of others, experiencing growth and development in self and others, parenting as a leader, and acquiring a sense of accomplishment throughout the process. Leadership is not simple, but one can be proficient at it. Effective leadership starts with having an understanding of leadership and ends with enjoyment in pearls of leadership. Good leaders make an impact and change lives within organizations on their level. The right leadership calls for a strategy for its success. Leadership is not simplistic, but with an understanding, leaders can overcome challenges within the process. Our society is calling for the right leadership both inside and outside organizations. Leaders need to examine themselves for behaviors that are causing them to stumble and fall short of effectively leading others. Leadership is not about leaders, but it is about those under their authority. Just serve the people!

Bibliography

2, A. (2018, December 20). *Inwards Advance Coaching.* Retrieved December 20, 2018, from https://inwards.gr/aksiologikes-ektimisis

3, A. (2008). "Diversity is not is not diversity". *INSEAD Articles*, n/a.

4, A. (1994). Fear of diversity. *Wall Street Journal, Europe Brussels*, 8.

5, A. (2009). See the person, Not the sterotype. *Southern Gazette*, 3.

Allen, S. J., & Hartman, N. S. (2008). Leadership development: An exploration of sources of learning. *S.A.M. Advanced Management Journal*, 10-19.

Alvesson, Mats, and Martin Blom. "Less followership, Less leadership? An inquiry into basic but seemingly forgotten downsides of leadership." *M@n@gement*, 2015: 266-282.

Amagoh, Francis. (2009). Leadership development and leadership effectiveness. *Management Decision*, 989-999.

Anonymous. (2006). What does it take to lead? *Healthcare Leadership Alliance; Healthcare Financial Management*, 78-81.

Anonymous, 6. (2007). Job gives them more than vocation. *Gulf News*, 1.

Anonymous, 7. (2003). A few pearls of wisdom. *JCK:Richmond*, 200-205.

Anonymous, 2. (1997). Should you be a consultant? 6 tips to help you decide. *Training*, S8.

Anonymous. "Why product managers don't cry over split milk." *Strategic Direction*, 2004: 22-24.

Anthony, Erica. (2017). The impact of leadership coaching on leadership behaviors. *The Journal of Management Development,* 930-939.

Arshavskiy, Marina. (2016). Great leadership. *Leadership Excellence Essentials*, 10-11.

Ashar, H., & Lane-Maher, M. (2004). Success and spirituality in the new business paradigm. *Journal of Management Inquiry*, 249-260.

Askew, O. A., Beister, J. M., & Keel, J. (2015). Current trends of unethical behavior within orgnaizations. *International Journal of Management & Information Systems (Online)*, 107-114.

Baker, K. F. (1967;1997). Hebrews 11-The promise of faith. *Review & Expositor*, 439-445.

Barker. (2003). Launch of the new leadership style for businesses. *Illawarra, Mercury*, 42.

Barmak, S. (2013). Building a better worker. *Maclean's*, 62.

Barram, M. D. (2003). Romans 12:9-21. *Interpretation*, 423-426.

Beeghly, E. (2015). What is a sterotype? What is sterotyping?. *Hypatia: Hoboken*, 675.

Bendall, Kim. "The seven basic principles of client report writing." *Professional Adviser*, 2014: 16-17.

Bhalla, Vikram, & Sebastian, Xavier. (2012). Navigation with a leadership compass. *Businessline*, 2012.

Boissoneau, R. (1986). Planning and conducting an information interview. *Hospital Materiel Management Quarterly*, 17.

Bostick, J. (2013). 'Everyone has that one personal struggle' Video. *McClathchy-Tribune Business News*, n/a.

Brandt, J. R. (2004). Parenting your company to profits. *Industry Week*, 23.

Braynion, Paula. (2004). Power and leadership. *Journal of Health Organization and Management*, 447-63.

Broad, M. (2005). Tough choices for a vocation. *Hosiptal Doctor*, 2.

Brown, M., Kulik, C. T., & Lim, V. (2016). Managerial tactics for communicating negative performance feedback. *Personnel Review*, 969-987.

Byron, W. J., & Gallagher, T. (2010). The church can learn a lot from 'servant leadership'. *National Catholic Reporter*, 26.

Caliqiuri, Paula. "Develop your cultural agility." *Training & Development*, 2013: 70-72.

Cangemi, Joesph P., and William Pfohl. "Sociopaths in high places." *Organization Development Journal*, 2009: 85-96.

Carroll, A. B. (2005). Servant leadership: An ideal for nonprofit organizations. *Nonprofit World*, 18-20.

Carter, Harry R. "Effective leaders check their egos at the door." *Firehouse*, 2006: 86-87.

Cashman, Kevin. (2010). Purpose Principle. *Leadership Excellence*, 7.

Castellano, S. (2015). A new yardstick captial index: Realizing the market value of leadership. *Talent Development*, 74.

Church, Alan H, and Janine Waclawski. *Organizational surveys: Designing and using: A seven-Step process.* San Francisco: Jossey-Bass, 2001.

Clutterbuck, David. "What's happening in coaching and mentoring? And what is the difference between them?" *Development and Learning in Organizations*, 2008: 8-10.

Coelho, Pedro S. "Creating customer loyalty through service customization." *European Journal of Marketing*, 2012: 331-356.

Cohen, W. (2018). Climbing the ladder of success. *Personal Excellence Essentials*, n/a.

Connock, Alex. (2015). Unlock your leadership passion. *INSEAD Articles*, n/a.

Cook, Sarah, & Macaulay, Steven. (2015). "Facing up to Blind-Spots." *Training Journal*, 46-49.

Cote, R. (2018). Dark side leaders: Are their intentions benign or toxic? *Journal of Leadership, Accountability and Ethics*, 42-65.

Covey, S. R. (1999). Unifying leadership. *Excecutive Excellence*, 3-4.

Cox, J. H. (2015). Closing talent development's knowing-Doing gap. *Talent Development*, 78-80.

Currin, D. (2008). Commentary: Lot Line: Building relationships. *Journal Record*, n/a.

Dean, Peter J. "Nine traits to look for in a mentor." *Agent's Sales Journal*, 2006: n/a.

Debeljak, Jelena, and Kristijan Krkac. ""Me, myself & I": practical egoism, selfishness, self-interest and business ethics." *Social Responsibility Journal*, 2008: 217-227.

Delia Davila Quintana, C., Mora Ruiz, J.-G., & Vila E., L. (2014). Competencies which shape leadership. *International Journal of Manpower*, 514-535.

Digh, P. (1998). Coming to terms with diversity. *HR Magazine*, 117-120.

Dizaho, E. K., Salleh, R., & Abdullah, A. (2017). Achieveing worklife balance through flexible work schedules and arrangements. *Global Business and Management Research, Suppl. Special Issue*, 455-465.

Dobbins, R., & Pettman, B. O. (1997). Give leadership. *Equal Opportunities International*, 19-29.

Dowd, S. E. (2000). Faith that works: James 2:14-26. *Review & Expositor*, 195-205.

Dreachslin, J. L. (2007). The role of leadership in creating a diversity-Sensitive organization. *Journal of Healthcare Management*, 151-5.

Drescher, G. (2017). Delegation outcomes: Perceptions of leaders and followers' satisfaction. *Journal of Managerial Psychology*, 2-15.

Du Plessis, T., & Van Viekerk, A. (2017). Factors influencing manager's attitudes towards performance appraisal. *SA Journal of Human Resource Management,* 1-10.

Duggan, K. (2018). Ethical blind spots. *Public Management,* 2-3.

Dyck, Dianne. "Internal and external consulting: Assisting clients with managing work, Health, And psychosocial issues." *AAOHN Journal,* 2002: 111-119.

Emerald Group Publishing Limited. "Leadership is about what we deliver: Shaping culture, Creating patterns of success." *Strategic Direction,* 2014: 24-26.

Epting, L. A., Glover, S. H., & Boyd, S. D. (1994). Managing diversity. *The Health Care Supervisor,* 73.

Ettorre, B. (1993). Diversity: Managing diversity for competitive advantage. *Management Review,* 6.

Fisher, J. R. (2006). Leadership as great ideas. *Leadership Excellence,* 14-15.

Francis-Smith, J. (2004). Surviving and thriving in the multigenerational workplace. *Journal Record,* 1.

French, Robert P.II. "The fuzziness of mindsets." *International Journal of Organizational Analysis,* 2016: 673-691.

Friday, E., & Friday, S. S. (2003). Managing diversity using a strategic planned change approach. *The Journal of Management Development,* 863-880.

Geedy, Nancy M. "Following a new roadmap to leadership success." *Nursing Management,* 2004: 49-51.

Galt, V. (2007). Cutthroat culture in decline. *The Globe and Mail.*

Garlington, D. B. (2010). 'Who is the greatest ?'. *Journal of the Evangelical Theological Society,* 287-316.

Gartner, Tony. "Commentary: Leaders are born, Not made..Or are they." *St. Charles County Business Record,* 2004: 1.

Garvey, Bob. "First-Person mentoring." *Career Development International,* 1996: 10-14.Gibb, S. (1994). Evaluating mentoring. *Education & Training,* 32.

Gaurav, Marathe, Girish Balasubramanian, and Manish Singhal. " Demystifying the leaderhip kaleidoscope into an intergrated view." *The Journal of Management Development*, 2017: 859-876.

Gibb, Stephen. "Evaluating mentoring." *Education & Training*, 1994: 32.

Gitomer, J. (2016). What's the reason some persist unitl they win and others quit? *Grand Rapids Business Journal*, 13.

Glazer, J. W. (1995). The call for leadership. *Journal of Leadership Studies*, 111-121.

Gowing, M. K., Morris, D. M., Seymour, A., & Gold, M. (2008). The next generation of leadership assessment: Some case studies. *Public Personnel Management*, 435-455.

Handysides, S. (2004). My struggles with personal development. *GP,* 21.

Hare, T. (2003). Fear in leadership: The adrenaline journey. *Training Journal,* 30.

Harris, Carol. "Consulting and you." *Consulting to Management*, 2010: 45-52.

Harrison, E. E. (2013). Executives leadership: Aligning passion and purpose. *Inside Counsel*, n/a.

Hawkins, Peter. "Developing an effective coaching strategy." *Global Focus*, 2009: 15-19.

Hayes, B. (2006). Keep smilin. *Rough Notes*, 118-119.

He, Yuangiong, Wenli Li, and Kin Keung Lai. "Service climate, Employee commitment and customer satisfaction." *International Journal of Contemporary Hospitality Management*, 2011: 592-607.

Hightower, H. J. (1983, August). Psychology at Florida Community College of Jacksonville. Jacksonville.

Hoerber, R. G. (1995). On the translation of Hebrews 11:1. *Concordia Journal*, 77-79.

Holton, Svetlana, and Joan Marques. "Empathy in Leadership: Appropriate or misplaced? An empirical study on a topic that is asking for attention." *Journal of Business Ethics*, 2012: 95-105.

Hoffman-Burdzinska, K., & Rutkowska, M. (2015). Work life balance as a factor influencing well-being. *Journal of Positive Management,* 87-101.

Hooijberg, Robert, Nancy Lane, and Albert Diverse. "Leader effectiveness and intergrity: Wishful thinking?." *International Journal of Organizational Analysis*, 2010: 59-75.

Hopkins, Willie E, Paul Mallette, and Shirley A. Hopkins. "Proposed factors influencing strategic inertial strategic renewal in organizations." *Academy of Strategic Management Journal*, 2013: 77-94.

Horne, Melissa. "Leadership Theory: Past, Present, and future." *Team Performance Management*, 1997: 270.

Huang, Y.-M. (2016). Networking behavior: From goal orientation to promotabilty. *Personnel Review*, 907-927.

Iordanoglou, Dimitra. "Future trends in leadership development practices and crucial leadership skills." *Journal of Leadership, Accountability and Ethics*, 2018: 118-129.

Jackson, P. (1998). Focus group interviews as a methodology. *Nurse Researcher,* 72.

Johnson Jr., E. S. (2000). Galatians 6:1-10. *Interpretation*, 300-302.

Kapoor, C., & Solomon, N. (2011). Understanding and managing generational differences in the workplace. *Worldwide Hospitality Tourism Themes,* 308-318.

Karp, Tom, and Thomas Helgo. "The future of leadership: The art of leading people in a " Post- Managerial" environment." *The Journal of Futures Studies, Strategic Thinking and Policy*, 2008: 30-37.

Kempster, Stephen. "Leadership learning through lived experience: A process of apprenticeship?" *Journal of Management and Organization*, 2006: 4-22.

Kennedy, Carol. (2000). "The Knowing-Doing Gap." *Directors*, 167.

Kerfoot, K. (2001). On leadership: From motivation to inspiration leadership. *Nursing Economics*, 242-243.

Khan, O. (2008). Liberating passion. *Leadership Excellence*, 12.

Khan, O. F., & Fazili, A. I. (2016). Work like balance: A conceptual review. *Journal of Strategic Human Resource*, 20-24.

Kilburn, B., & Cates, T. (2010). Leader behavior: Gate keeper to voluntary upward feedback. *Management Research Review*, 900-910.

Kilgallen, J. J. (2003). Marta and mary: Why at Luke 10:38-42? *Biblica*, 555.

Kirkpatrick, D. l. (2012). Intergrating training and performance appraisal. *Training*, 12-13.

Kirkwood, J. J. (2016). How women and men business oweners perceive success. *International Journal of Entrepreneurial Behavior & Research*, 594-615.

Kirsch, A. (2018). Does honor matter? *Yerepouni Daily News*, n/a.

Lawn, John. "What is leadership?" *Food Management*, 2013: 6.

Lawrence, P. (2015). Building great 360 feedback program. *Training & Development*, 5-7.

Leider, R. J. (2008). The leader in midlife. *Business Strategy Series*, 115-118.

Lenz, T. (2013). Networking as a leadership habit. *Public Administration Review*, 364.

Lopez, L. (2008). An honorable life is a goal for us all. *Tampa Tribune*, 2.

MacFadden, D. (2003). A guide to resume references [Final Edition]. *Alberni Valley Times*, 17.

MacGibbon, M. (2011). Never give into fear. *SuperVision*, 9-10.

Maher Jr., J. H., & Kur, E. C. (1983). Constructing good questionnaires. *Training and Development Journal*, 100.

Maidique, Modesto A, and Nathan J. Hiller. "The mindsets of a leader." *MIT Sloan Management Review*, 2018: 76-81.

Marques, Joan. "The changed leadership landscape: What matters today." *The Journal of Management Development*, 2015: 1310--1322.

McDemott, Mike, Alec Levenson, and Suzanne Newton. "What coaching can and cannot do for your organization." *HR. Human Resources Planning*, 2007: 30-37.

McKnight, William. *90 days to success in consulting*. Boston: Cengage Learning, 2010.

Mathews, C. (2007). Forgingties: How to build solid relationships. *CIO Canada*, N_A.

Maurer, T. J., & Lippstrey, M. (2008). Who will be committed to an organization that provides support for employee development ? *The Journal of Management Development*, 328-347.

Maxwell, G. A., Blair, S., & McDougall, M. (2001). Edging towards managing diversity in practice. *Employee Relations*, 468-482.

McCall Jr., M. W., & Lombardo, M. M. (1982). Using simulation for leadership and management research: Through the looking glass. *Management Science (pre-1986)*, 533.

McConnell, E. A. (2001). Compentence Vs. competency. *Nursing Management*, 14.

McDemott, M., Levenson, A., & Newton, S. (2007). What coaching can and cannot do for your organization. *HR. Human Resources Planning*, 30-37.

McKnight, W. (2010). *90 days to success in consulting*. Boston: Cengage Learning.

Molinaro, V. (2015). Driving leadership accountability: A critical business priority for hr leaders. *People and Strategy*, 32-36.

Morgan, D. L. (1996). Focus groups. *Annual Review of Sociology*, 129-152.

Navarro, A. (2011). Good networking /Bad networking. *Physician Executive*, 58-60.

New, G. (2014). The voice: From text to life-The one thing. *Stimulus*, 32-35.

Newbigin, L. (1993). Certain Faith: What kind of certainty?. *Tyndale Bulletin*, 339-350.

Newstex. "Coaching tips: The leadership blog: Leadership mindset." *Newstex, Global Business Blogs*, 2014.

Northouse, Peter G. *Leadership : Theory and practice: Six edition.* New Delhi: SAGE Publications, Inc., 2013.

Olson, David A. "Are great leaders born, Or are they made?" *Frontiers of Health Services Management*, 2009: 27-30.

Overell, S. (2005). You should reap what you sow. *Personnel Today*, 13.

Pace, M. (2017). The strength of faith and trust. *International Journal for Philosophy of Religion*, 135-150.

Patten, R. M. (2003). Link people, Strategy, And performance. *Executive Excellence*, 20.

Perkins, D. W. (1986). The wisdom we need:James 1:5-8,3:13-18. *The Theological Educator*, 17-25.

Pfay, B., Kay, I., Nowack, K. M., & Ghorpade, J. (2002). Does 360-Degree feedback program negatively affect company performance? *HR Magazine*, 54-59.

Pfeffer, J., & Sutton, R. I. (2000). *The knowing-Doing gap: How smart companies turn knowledge into action.* Boston: Harvard Business School Publishing.

Polat, S., & Sonmez, B. (2018). The correlation between the power styles used by nurse managers and bullying behavior. *International Journal of Organizational Leadership*, 84-98.

Pplboon, Nuntamanop, Ilkka Kauranen, and Barbara Igel. "A new model of strategic thinking competency." *Journal of Strategy and Management*, 2013: 242-264.

Qyinlade, A. O. (2006). A method of assessing leadership effectiveness: Introducing the essential behavioral leadership qualities approach. *Performance Improvement*, 25-40.

Reyes, Liske: Jessica M, and Courtney L. Holladay. "Evaluating coaching's effect:Competencies, Career mobility and retention." *Leadership & Organization Development Journal*, 2016: 936-948.

Riess, J. K. (1997). The woman of worth: Impressions of Proverbs 31:10-31. *Dialogue*, 141-151.

Robertson, Larry. (2005). The cost of misssed opportunities. *Strategic Communication Management*, 5.

Robertson, Christopher, and Scott Geiger. "Moral philosophy and managerial perceptions of ethics codes." *Cross Cultural Management*, 2011: 351-365.

Rockwell, Dan. (2016). "Leadership Freak: The top 12 missed opportunities of leadership." *Weblog Post: Newstex Global Business Blogs*.

Rodgers, J. O. (1993). Implementing a diversity strategy. *LIMRA'S MarketFacts*, 26.

Rolfe, Ann. "How to design your mentoring program." *Training and Development in Australia*, 2008: 32-34.

Rowley, J. (2006). What do we know about wisdom? *Management Decision*, 1246-1257.

Ruggero, E., & Haley, D. F. (2005). *The leader's compass: 2nd Edition*. King of Prussia: Academy Leadership.

Schein, Edgar H. *Organizational culture and leadership*. San Francisco: Jossey-Bass, 2010.

Silva, Alberto. "What is leadership?" *Journal of Business Studies Quarterly*, 2016: 1-5.

Shannon, S. (2017). The long fall and curious rise of the pearl industry. *FT.com*, n/a.

Simons, A. (2009). Changing workplace demographics: T+B+Y+X=Opportunity. *CPA Practice Management Forum*, 15-16,23.

Sonnenberg, Frank K. "Cultivating Creativity." *Executive Excellence*, 1991: 13.

Stagg, F. (1911-2001; 1991). Galatians 6:7-10. *Review & Expositor*, 247-251.

Stettner, M. (2014). Lead better by asking for feedback. *Investor's Business Daily*, A07.

Stewart, N. (pre 1986:1960). Free yourself of blind spots: Five steps will help you overcome mental blocks to success. *Nation's Business*, 86.

Stieber, Gus. "A rx for problems affecting job performance: EAPs." *ACA News*, 1999: 41-43.Stiffney, R. (2010). Leadership as landscaping. *The Journal of Applied Christian*, 95-105.

Stiffney, Rick. "Leadership as landscaping." The Journal of Applied Christian, 2010: 95-105.

Suarez, G. J. (1996). Managing fear. *Excellence*, 8.

Sudha, K. S., Shahnawaz, M., & Farhat, A. (2016). Leadershhip styles, Leader's effectiveness and well-being: Exlporing collective efficacy as a mediator. *Vision*, 111-120.

Sutton, R., Pfeffer, J., & Anonymous. (2000). The knowing-doing gap: How smart companies turn knowledge into action. *Food Management*, 13.

Temkin, T. (2009). Diversity, Diversity, Everyone wants diversity. *Nonprofit World*, 6-7.

Thompson, P. (2015). Leadership diversity: The path to value-Base care. *Hospital & Health Networks*, 41-51.

Tisch, J. M. (2004). From 'Me' Leadership to 'We' Leadership. *Wall Street Journal (Eastern Edition)*, B2.

Todaro, Julie. "Mentoring: Advice from an expert." *Library Leadership & Management (Online)*, 2011: 1-7.

Tucker, Bruce A, and Robert F. Russell. "The influence of the transformational leader." *Journal of Leadership & Organizational*, 2004: 103-111.

Underwod, Chris. "Purpose in leadership," Training Journal, 2016: 30-32.

Van der Does, Louise, and Stephen J. Calderia. "Effective leaders champion communication skills." Nation's Restaurant News, 2006: 20-28.

Veith, Gene Edward. "Vocation: The theology of the Christian life." Journal of Markets and Morality, 2011: n/a.

Visagie, Jan, Herman Linde, and Werner Havenga. "Leadership competencies for managing diversity." Managing Transitions, 2011: 225-247.

Warden, Gail. "Leadership diversity." Journal of Healthcare Management, 1999: 421-2.

Warnek, Jon. "In midst of suffering, Christ is there." The Billings Gazette, 2017: n/a.

Wheatley, Margaret J. "Spiritual leadership." Executive Excellence, 2002: 5-6.

WeblogPost. "Leadership freak: Stop pushing-Create pull." *Newstex Global Business*, 2015: n/a.

Welsh, Elizabeth Torney, Devasheesh Bhave, and Kyoung Young Kim. "Are you my mentor ? Informal mentoring mutual identification." *Career Development International*, 2012: 137-148.

White, Dana. "How to truly lead: And not simply manage." *Leadership Excellence Essentials*, 2016: 21.

Zabriskie, Kate. "Using the power of " Thank you" to get what you want: Influencing others made easier." *Personal Excellence Essentials*, 2018: n/a.

Zach, Melusen. "Opinion: Sterotyping organizations leads to unfair judgment." University Wire, 2018.

Zenger, Jack, and Kathleen Stinnett. "Why Coach?" *Leadership Excellence,* 2007: 20.

Zuber, Franziska. "Spread of unethical behavior in organizations: A dynamic social network perspective." Journal of Business Ethics, 2015: 151-172.

Appendix

Executive Summary

Most customers are expecting great experiences in service industries since they are paying out of their pockets. There is a direct connection between customer service and customer satisfaction. [546] However, to determine if both are being achieved, organizations must assess its culture for efficiency and effectiveness, which is an ongoing process for leaders. How is this performed? It can be done through feedback from customers and employees using an instrument tool. Successful organizations are continuously making changes and looking from areas of opportunities within their establishments. "Most organizations understand that customers do not want more choices; customers want exactly what they want, when, where and how they want it, and technology now makes it possible for organizations to give it to them."[547]

---

[546] Yuangiong He, Wenli Li, and Kin Keung Lai, "Service Climate, Employee Commitment and Customer Satisfaction," *International Journal of Contemporary Hospitality Management* (2011): 593.

[547] Pedro S. Coelho, "Creating Customer Loyalty through Service Customization," *European Journal of Marketing* (2012): 351.

Background

Dear sir:

Thank you for reading this customer's report generated by Linda. The purpose of this report is to discuss my experience while traveling through the airport. The experience was frightening, and I do not want any other customer to share my experiences. In the past, I have dreaded traveling through this airport, but I really did not understand why until recently. I really enjoying flying. The first flight was a short flight—no problems with the airline. However, when I entered the airport, I was totally confused and frightened. I saw the monitor to the right of the entrance way, but I did not see signage to proceed to the next gate.

After locating my next gate, I looked to the left and I found no signage. I looked to the right, and I saw signage down the hall from a distance, but I really could not read it. So I decided to follow the crowd of people moving to the right, and I was lost. From this point, my experience did not improve. On the return flight, I decided to take a different approach; I did not want to have a dreading feeling again. So, I decided to write down some observations and send them to you, in order to improve the customer's experience.

Problem

- ☐ Construction being done on the upper interior surface (ceiling) presented a feeling of unsafety for customers.
- ☐ Signage is outdated for the current renovation situation.
- ☐ The flow of people was chaotic and confusing; people and vehicles are moving toward each other.
- ☐ Exits are not recognizable in an emergency, placing customers at risk.
- ☐ There are too many people in one area, bottlenecks at some points, no customer service representatives for help.

Recommendations

These are some recommendations to enhance services being provided by the airport to improving customers' experiences.

1. **Most important: update current signage to the current state of the business.** Signage is a form of communication for everyone, hearing impaired, visually impaired. I did not struggle with where I had to go but how to get there. The signage was unclear and confusing. I had to turn around several times since I was lost, no signage on the second floor using the escalator. Having signage that is outdated places everyone at risk. Even signage that reads, "Please pardon our construction. Growth in progress" is useful.

2. **Customer services representative visibility.** With thousands of people traveling through your organizations daily, questions are inevitable. People need answers and assistance throughout the hours. How could people *quickly identify* who is working for customer services? It can be done by allowing your staff to wear a yellow blouse or shirt (or another color that stands out). Wearing a vest is not reliable since staff can forget to place it on. Wearing neutral colors create blending with customers.

3. **Mapping for customers upon exiting and entering terminals, especially near monitors.** For instance, maps can read, "You are here and you want to go A-Z. Take this train (or escalator) to get there." Your organization can not assume that all customers are familiar with the layout of the airport. This can improve people flow.

4. **People flow.** There needs to be a strategic plan created to improve movement throughout the airport. The observation for movement included people, vehicles, wheelchairs, and luggage. A design for lane flow on the flooring might be beneficial. For instance, a design showing three lanes, the middle lane is for moving vehicles, wheelchairs, emergency staff, and personnel working on flights. Everyone else can stay to the right of both lanes, walking in the same direction but on

opposite sides. This will reduce some of the chaos.

5. **Role reversal for leadership.** Become a customer and go through the entire process as a customer, not judging your system but looking for areas of opportunities; walking in the customer's shoes can be insightful.

Conclusion

Thank you for allowing me to share my experiences. I hope this will positively impact change. I can see all the work being done already to make things better for customers, such as the concession areas. It is good to know that some organizations are still willing to listen to their customer's perspective.

Linda concluded the report with her contact information. She was hoping that leadership would contact for follow-up, but it never occurred. Months later, Linda had learned that the airport experienced a power failure, causing hundreds of people to be stranded without lights in a dark airport for hours. Linda felt so bad for those customers, but she was glad not to have been there. Linda had learned that customer services wore shirts for quick identification during the power outage, maybe they read and listened to Linda's words.

CPSIA information can be obtained
at www.ICGtesting.com
Printed in the USA
BVHW032144041020
590294BV00001B/4